NICKELODEON

降去神通

AVATAR

THE LAST AIRBENDER™

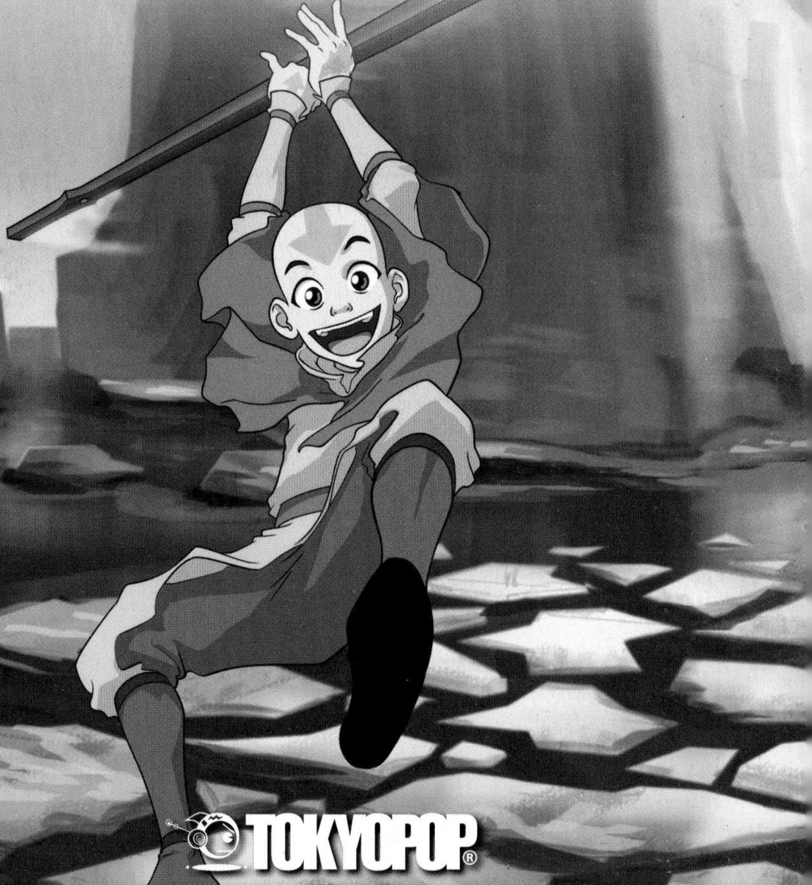

TOKYOPOP®

Hamburg • London • Los Angeles • Tokyo

Editor - Zachary Rau
Contributing Editor - Robert Langhorn
Graphic Designer, Letterer & Cover Designer - Tomás Montalvo-Lagos
Graphic Artists - Anna Kernbaum, John Lo and Monalisa J. de Asis

Digital Imaging Manager - Chris Buford
Production Managers - Jennifer Miller and Mutsumi Miyazaki
Senior Designer - Anna Kernbaum
Senior Editor - Elizabeth Hurchalla
Managing Editor - Lindsey Johnston
VP of Production - Ron Klamert
Publisher & Editor in Chief - Mike Kiley
President & C.O.O. - John Parker
C.E.O. - Stuart Levy

E-mail: info@TOKYOPOP.com
Come visit us online at www.TOKYOPOP.com

A ⬧TOKYOPOP Cine-Manga® Book
TOKYOPOP Inc.
5900 Wilshire Blvd., Suite 2000
Los Angeles, CA 90036

Avatar: The Last Airbender Chapter 2

ISBN: 1-59816-918-1

First TOKYOPOP® printing: May 2006

10 9 8 7 6 5 4 3 2 1

Printed in the USA

NICKELODEON

降去神通
AVATAR
THE LAST AIRBENDER

CREATED BY
MICHAEL DANTE DIMARTINO &
BRYAN KONIETZKO

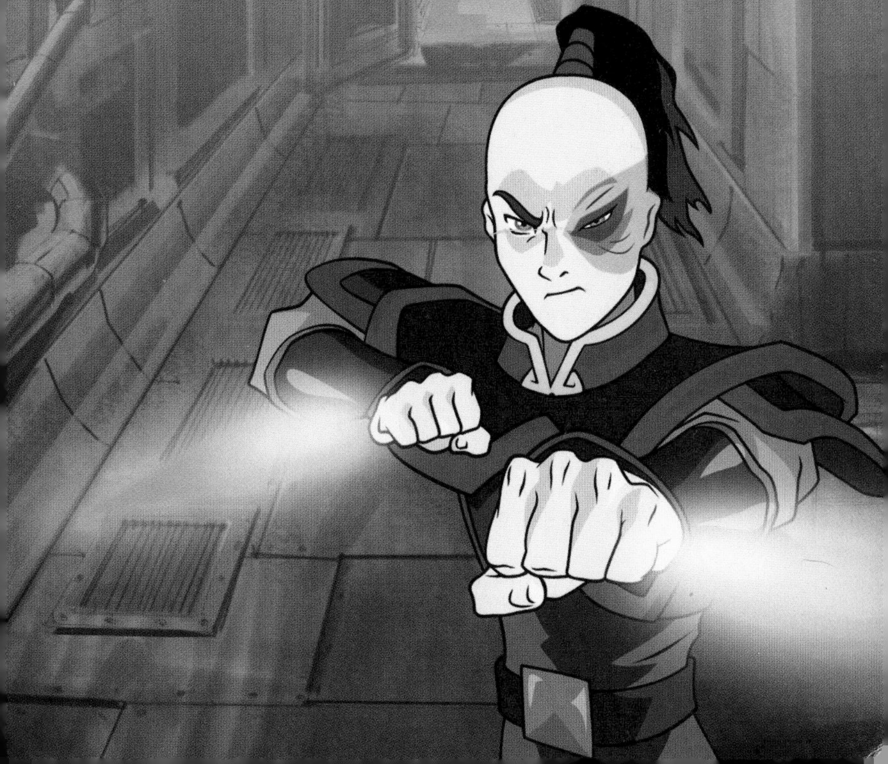

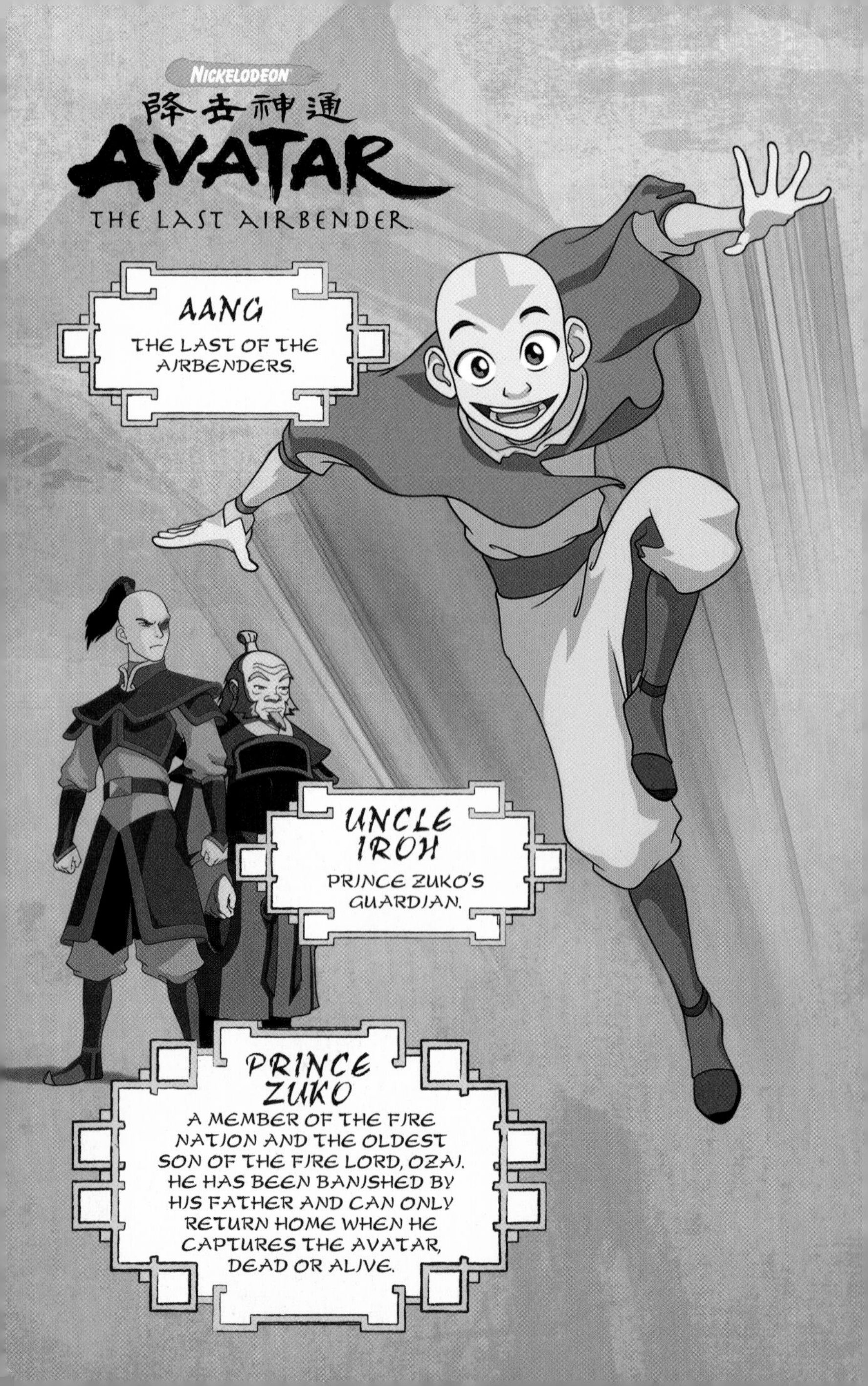

NICKELODEON
降去神通
AVATAR
THE LAST AIRBENDER
AANG
THE LAST OF THE AIRBENDERS.
UNCLE IROH
PRINCE ZUKO'S GUARDIAN.
PRINCE ZUKO
A MEMBER OF THE FIRE NATION AND THE OLDEST SON OF THE FIRE LORD, OZAI. HE HAS BEEN BANISHED BY HIS FATHER AND CAN ONLY RETURN HOME WHEN HE CAPTURES THE AVATAR, DEAD OR ALIVE.

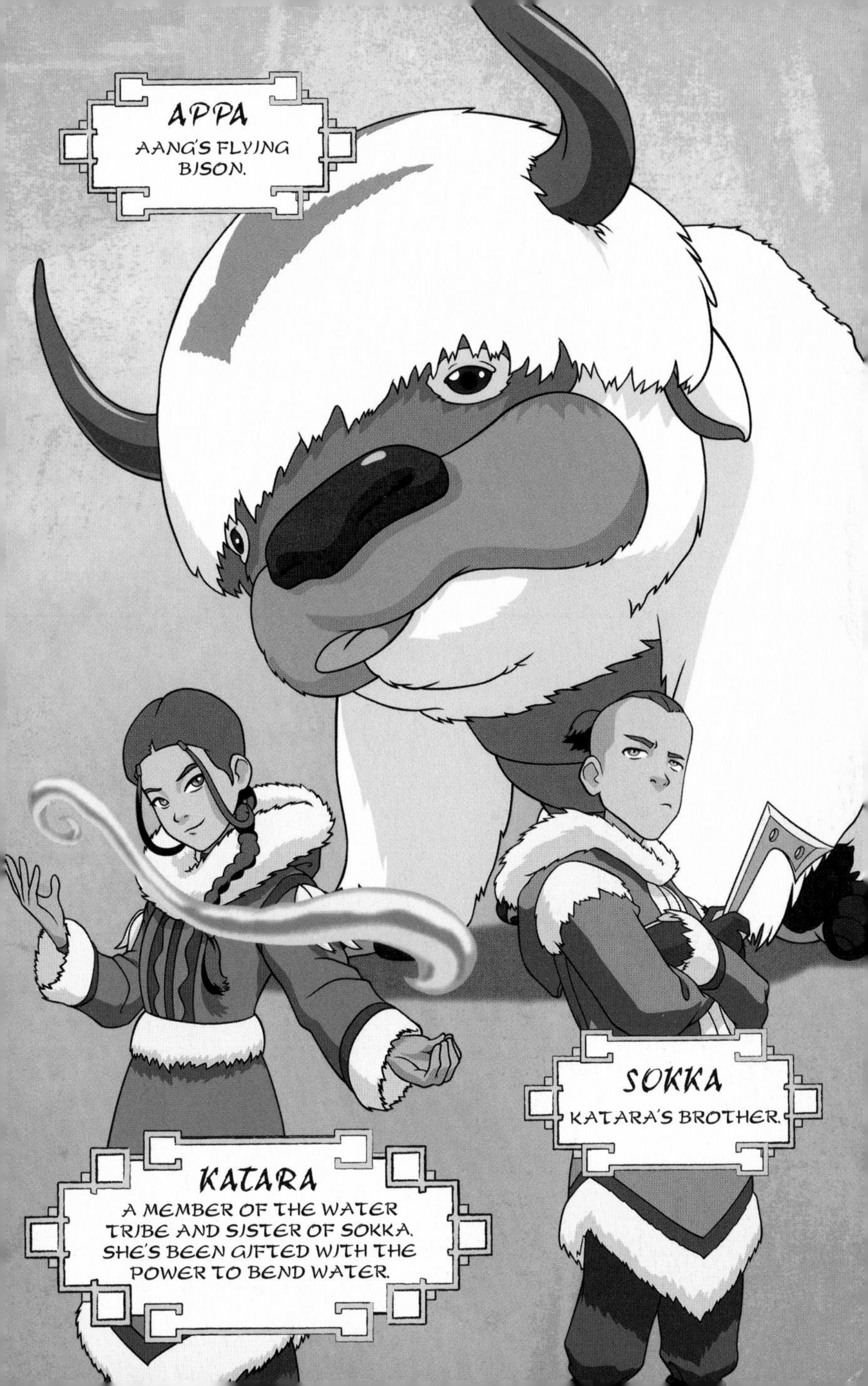
APPA
AANG'S FLYING BISON.
SOKKA
KATARA'S BROTHER.
KATARA
A MEMBER OF THE WATER TRIBE AND SISTER OF SOKKA. SHE'S BEEN GIFTED WITH THE POWER TO BEND WATER.

NICKELODEON

降去神通

AVATAR

THE LAST AIRBENDER

CHAPTER 2:
CONTENTS

THE STORY SO FAR...

WHILE OUT FISHING, KATARA AND HER BROTHER SOKKA DISCOVER A YOUNG BOY CALLED AANG AND HIS FLYING BISON, APPA, TRAPPED IN AN ICEBERG. BREAKING HIM OUT OF HIS FROZEN PRISON, THEY LEARN THAT HE IS AN AIRBENDER AND HAS BEEN TRAPPED IN THE ICE FOR A HUNDRED YEARS.

THE GROUP RETURNS TO THE WATER TRIBE'S VILLAGE, NOT KNOWING THAT FREEING AANG HAS ALERTED A FIRE NAVY WARSHIP CARRYING THE TERRIBLE PRINCE ZUKO.

NOW PRINCE ZUKO KNOWS THE SECRET LOCATION OF THE WATER VILLAGE AND IS ON HIS WAY TO DESTROY IT. WILL SOKKA, KATARA AND AANG FIND OUT IN TIME TO SAVE THE VILLAGE?

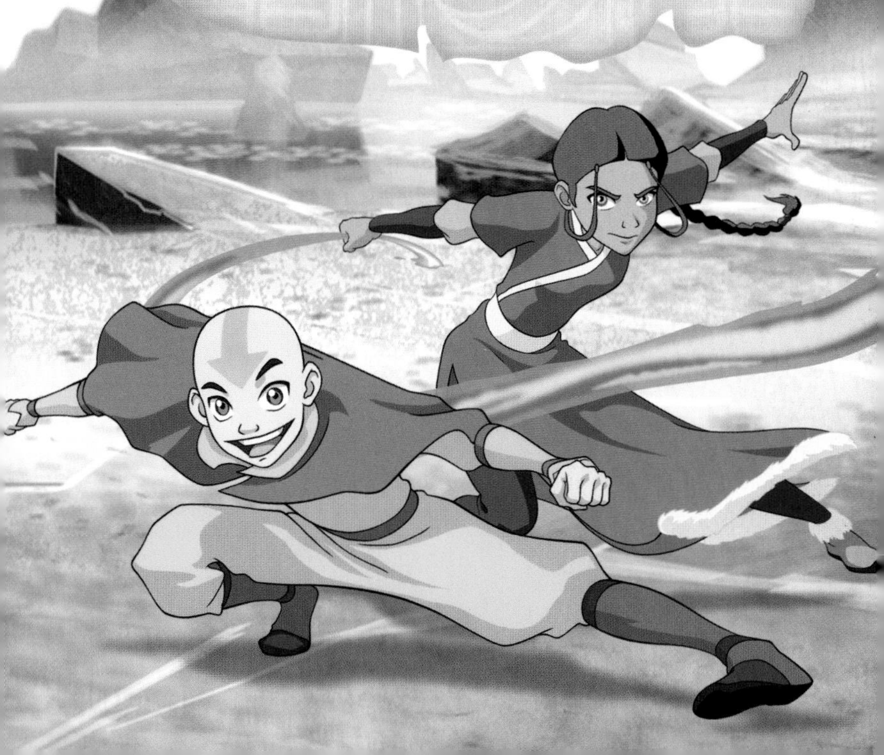

THE AVATAR RETURNS

WRITTEN BY
MICHAEL DANTE DIMARTINO
& BRYAN KONIETZKO

ADDITIONAL WRITING BY
AARON EHASZ, PETER GOLDFINGER
AND JOSH STOLBERG

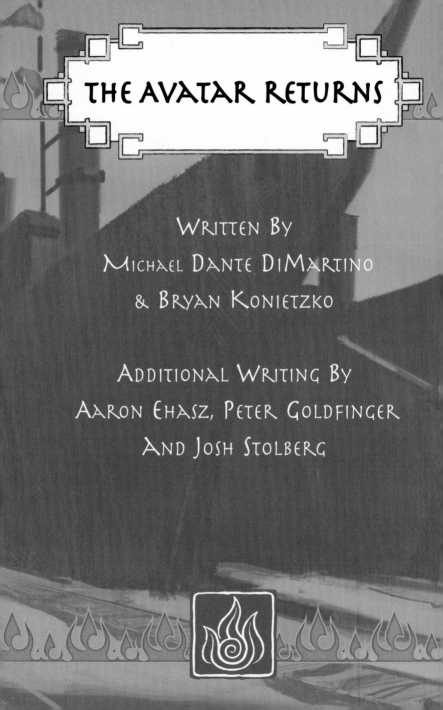

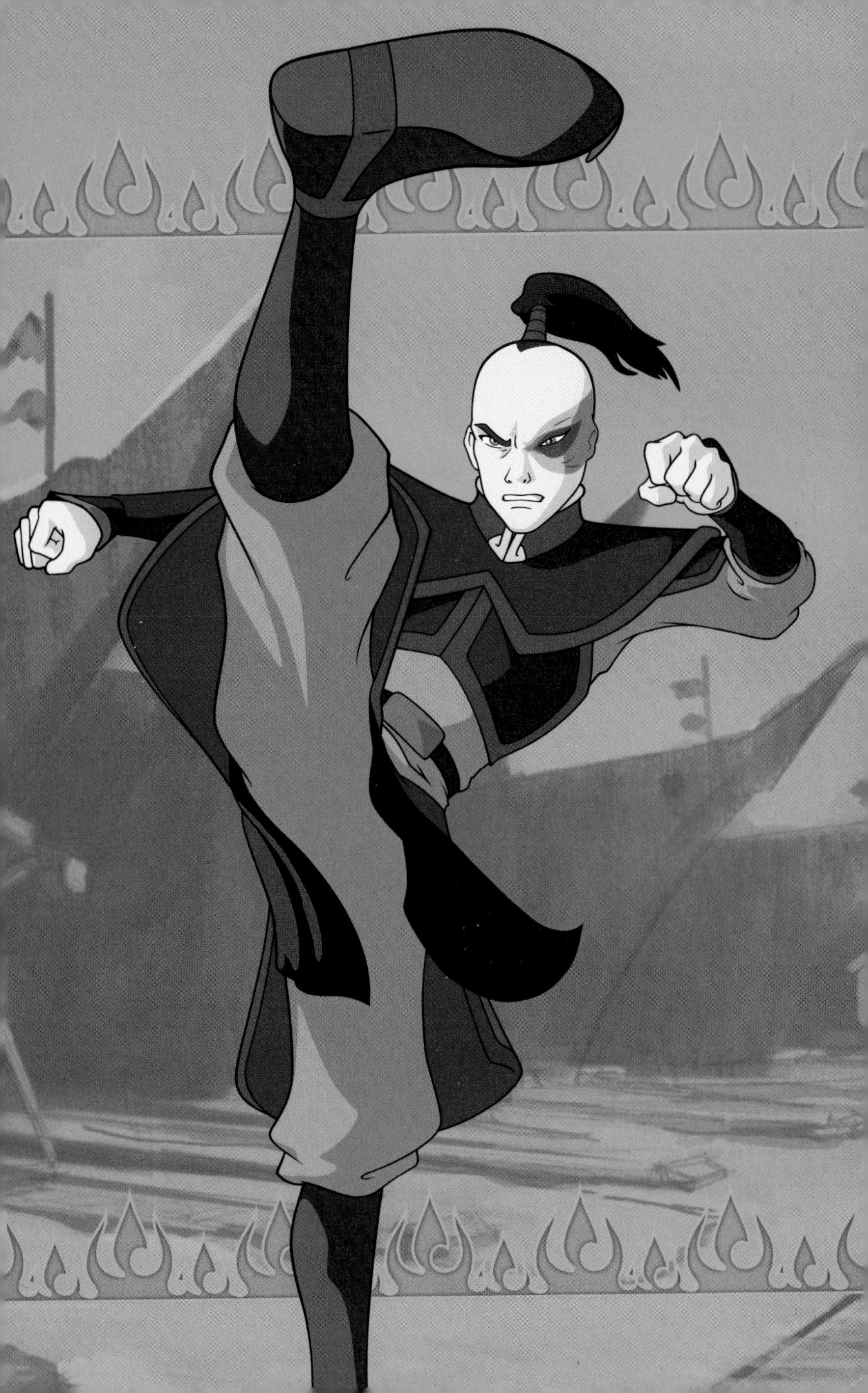

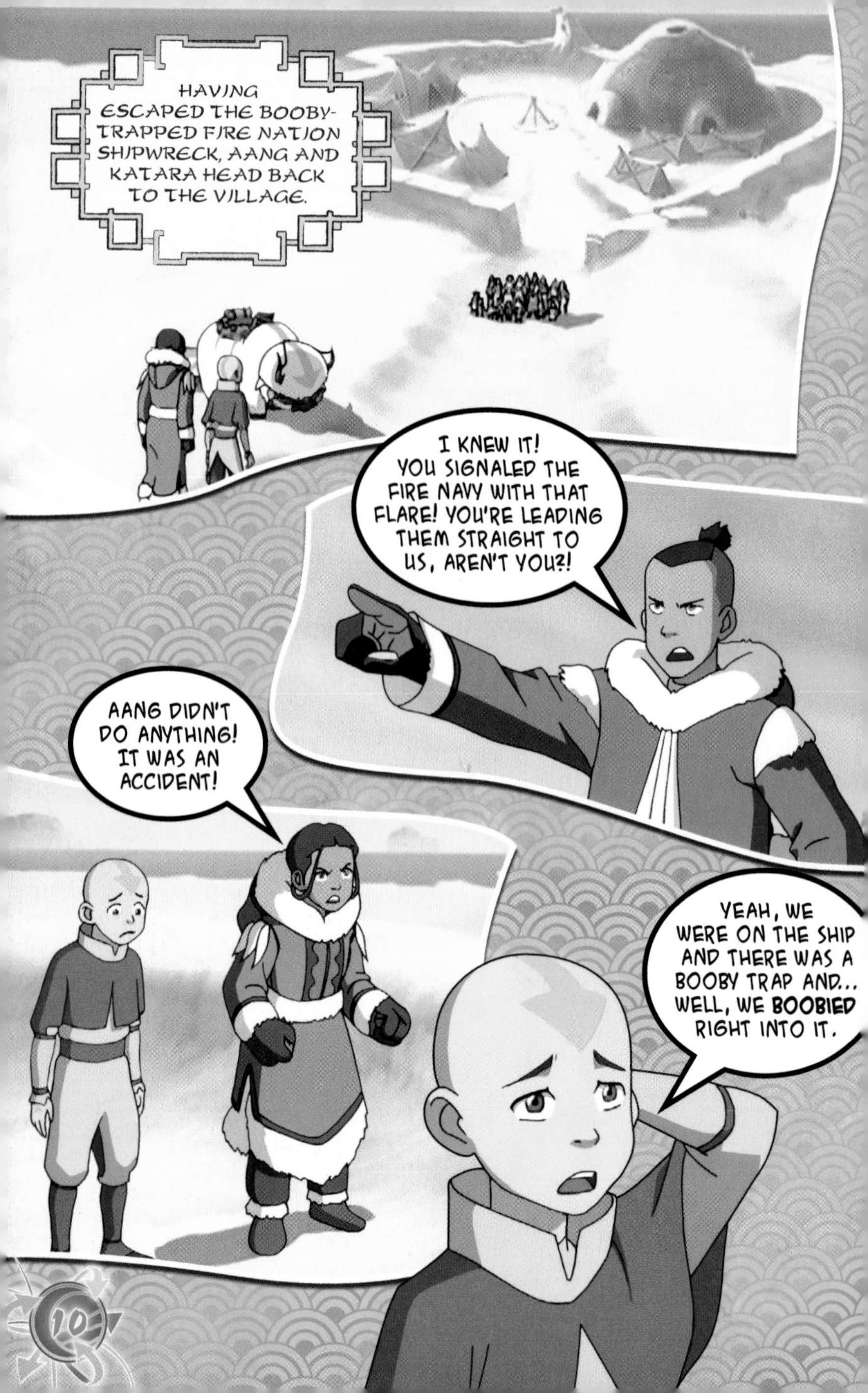
HAVING ESCAPED THE BOOBY-TRAPPED FIRE NATION SHIPWRECK, AANG AND KATARA HEAD BACK TO THE VILLAGE.
I KNEW IT! YOU SIGNALED THE FIRE NAVY WITH THAT FLARE! YOU'RE LEADING THEM STRAIGHT TO US, AREN'T YOU?!
AANG DIDN'T DO ANYTHING! IT WAS AN ACCIDENT!
YEAH, WE WERE ON THE SHIP AND THERE WAS A BOOBY TRAP AND... WELL, WE **BOOBIED** RIGHT INTO IT.

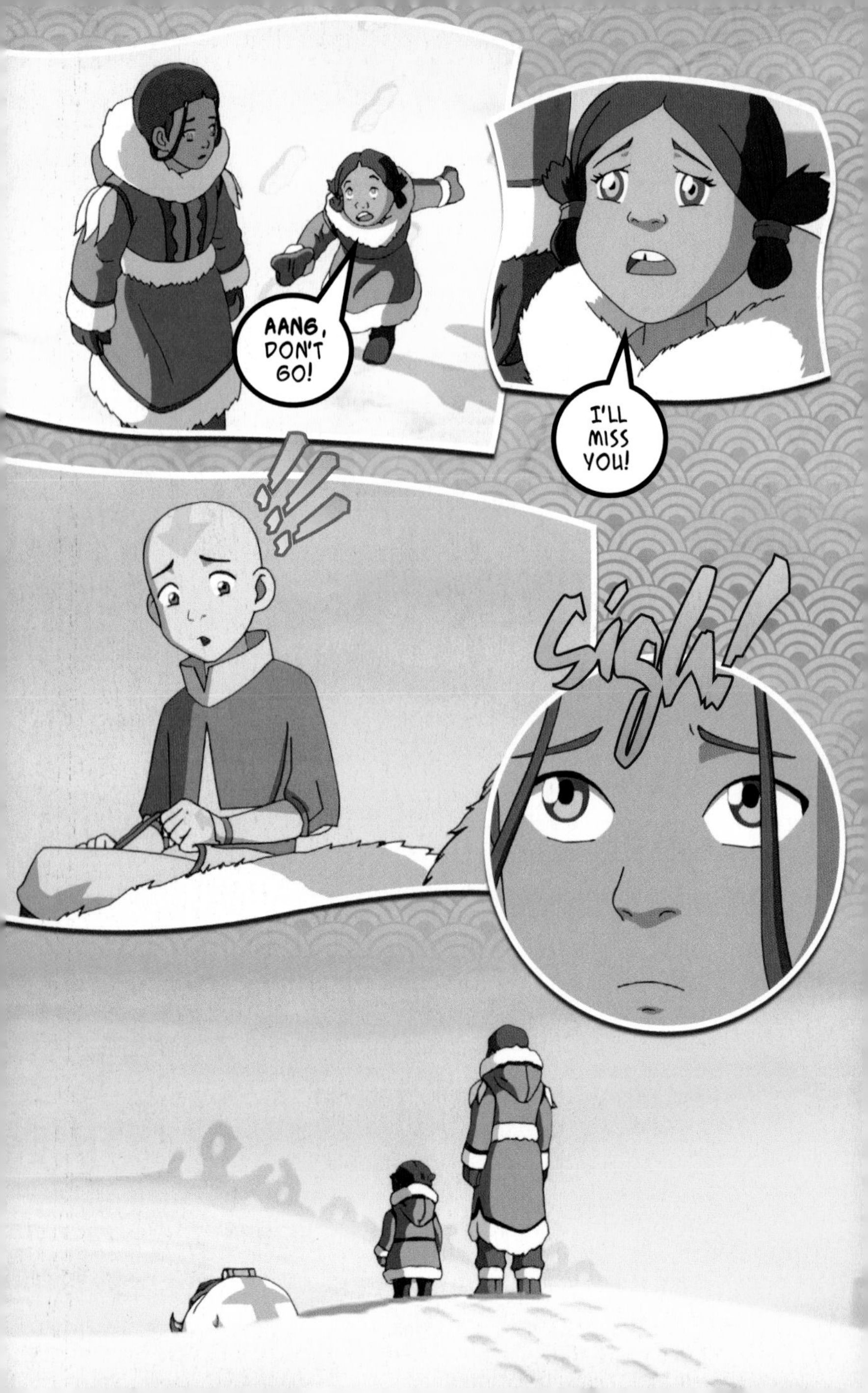
AANG, DON'T GO!
I'LL MISS YOU!
Sigh!

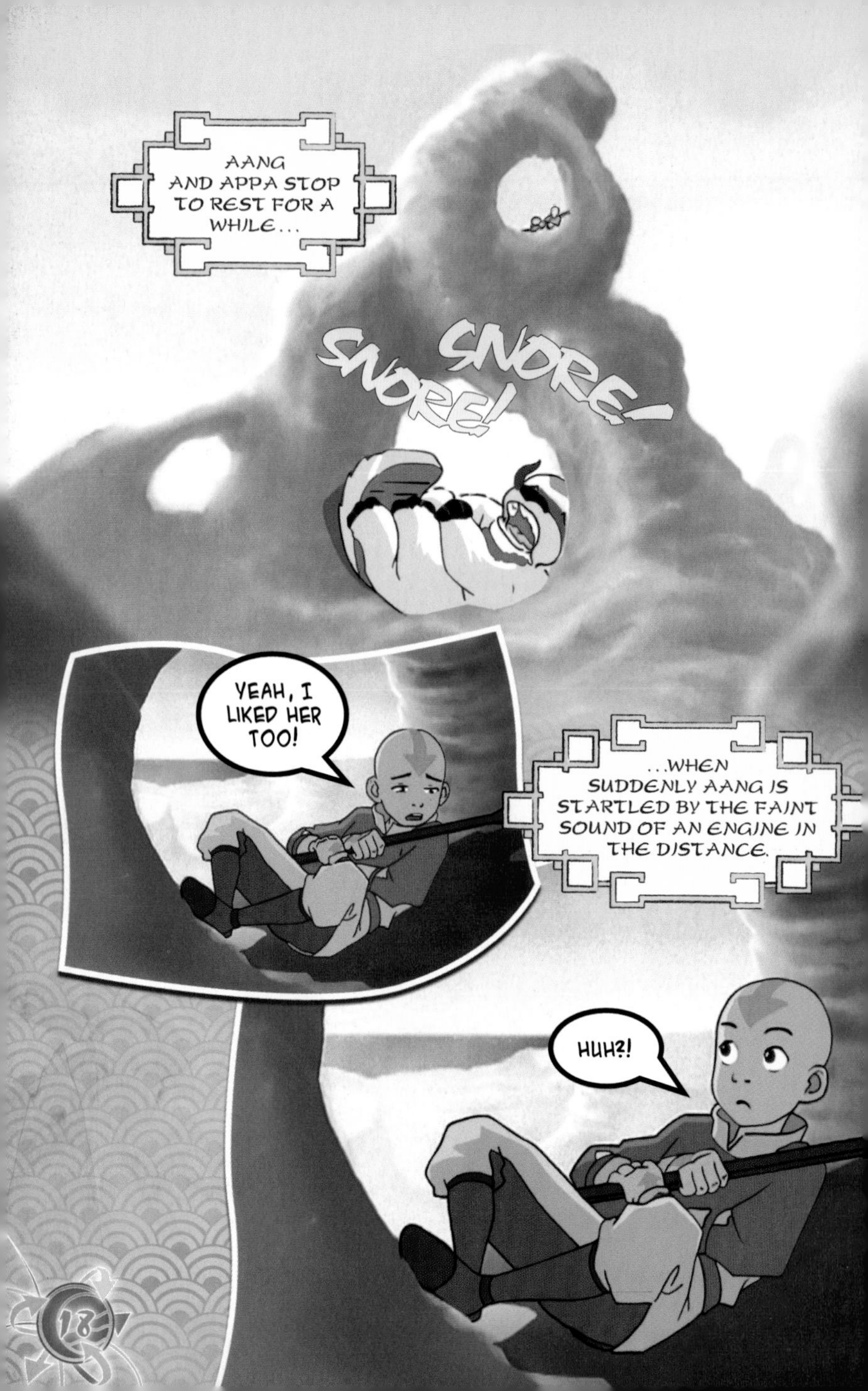

AANG AND APPA STOP TO REST FOR A WHILE...
SNORE! SNORE!
YEAH, I LIKED HER TOO!
...WHEN SUDDENLY AANG IS STARTLED BY THE FAINT SOUND OF AN ENGINE IN THE DISTANCE.
HUH?!

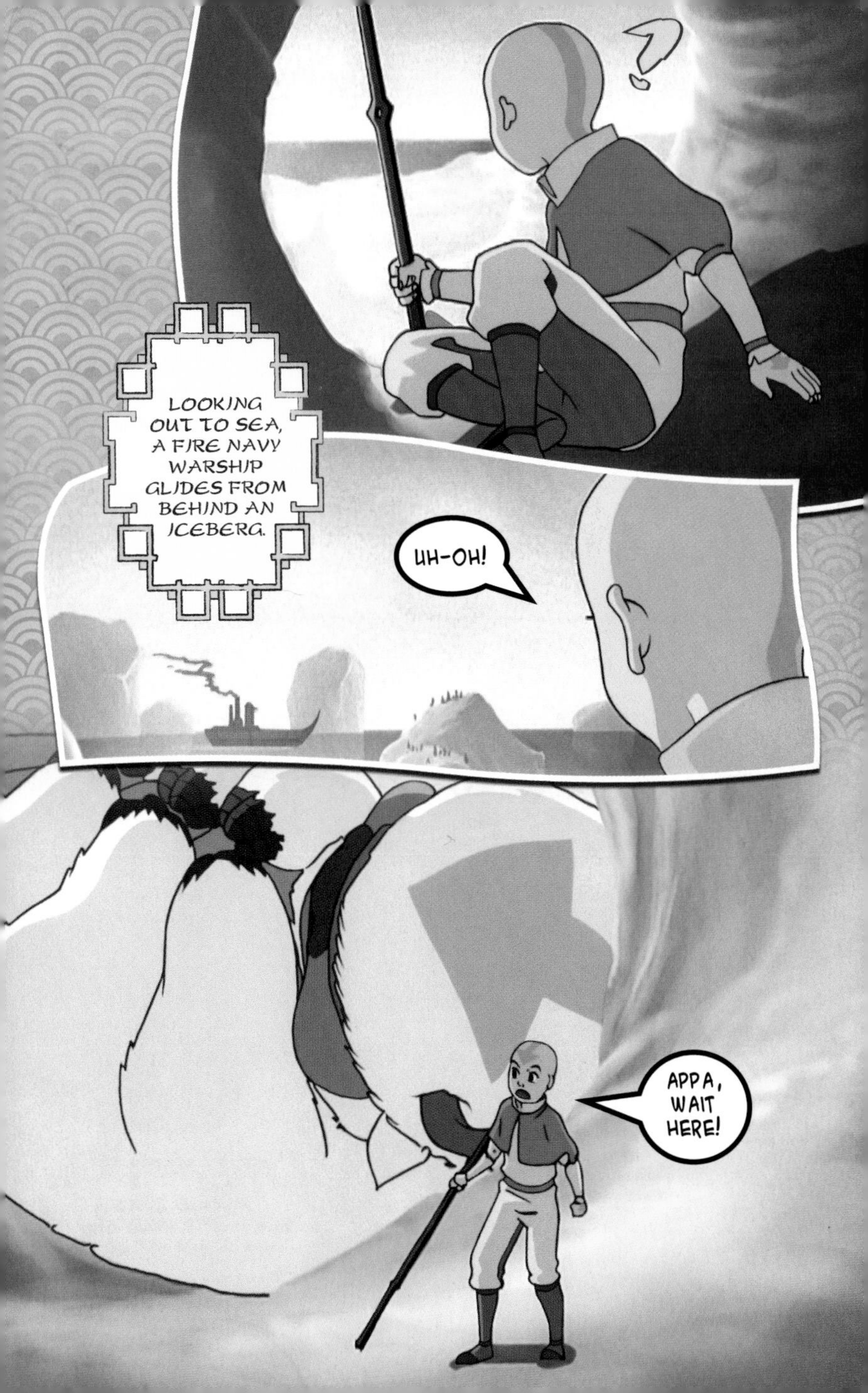

LOOKING OUT TO SEA, A FIRE NAVY WARSHIP GLIDES FROM BEHIND AN ICEBERG.
UH-OH!
APPA, WAIT HERE!

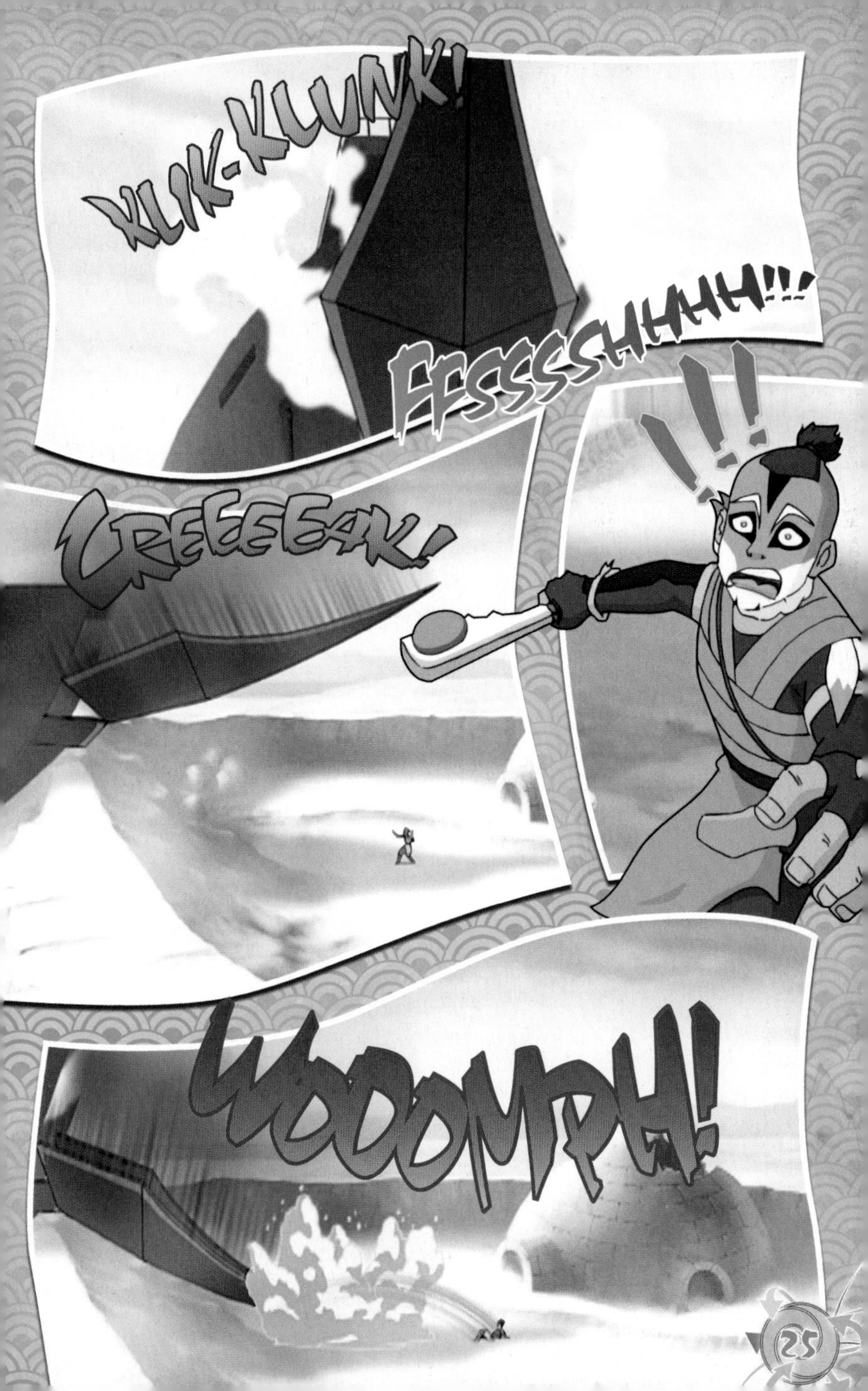
KLIK-KLUNK!
FFSSSSHHHHH!!!
CREEEEAK!
!!!
WOOOMPH!

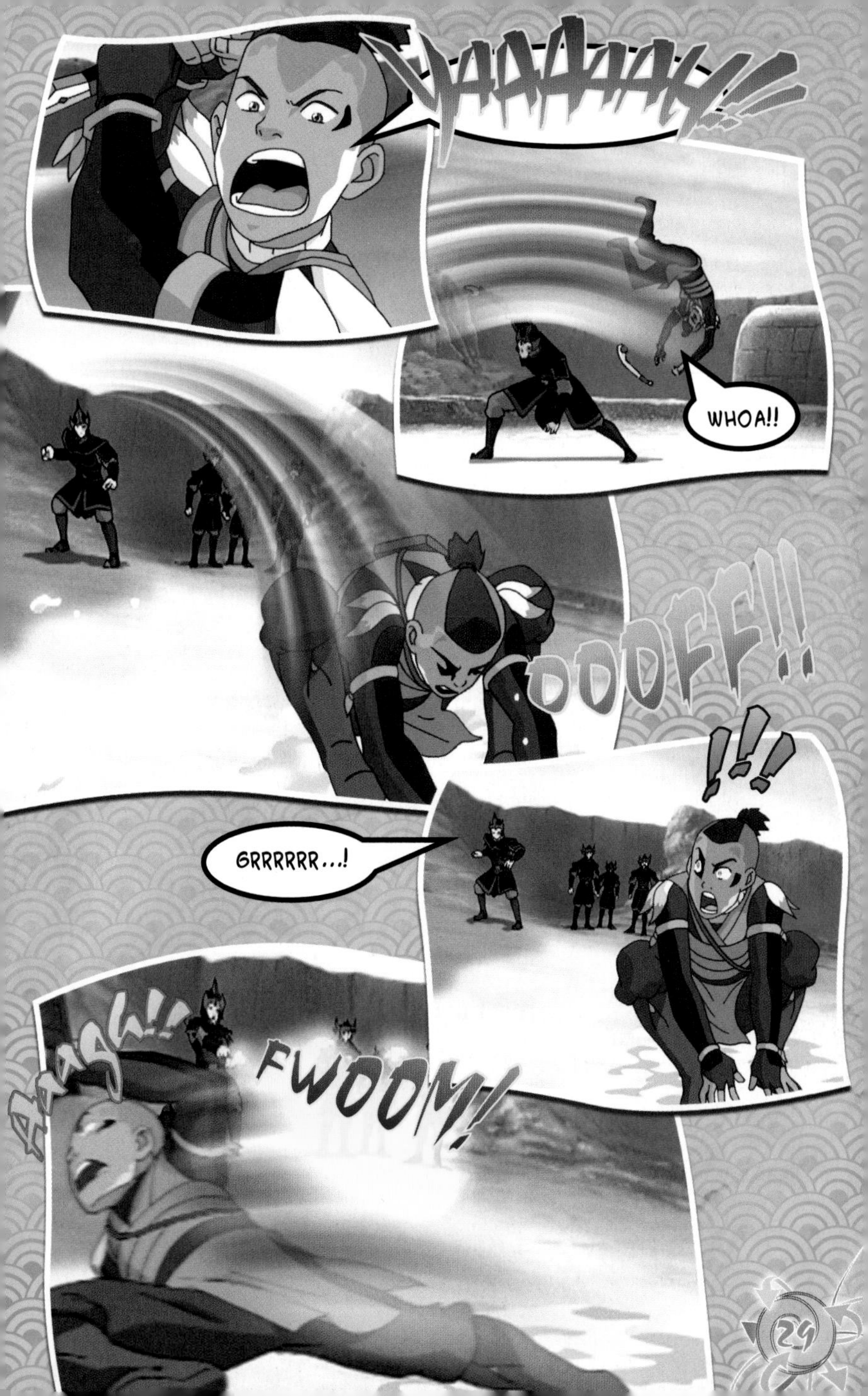
YAAAAAH!!
WHOA!!
OOOFF!!
GRRRRRR...!
!!!
AAAGH!!
FWOOM!

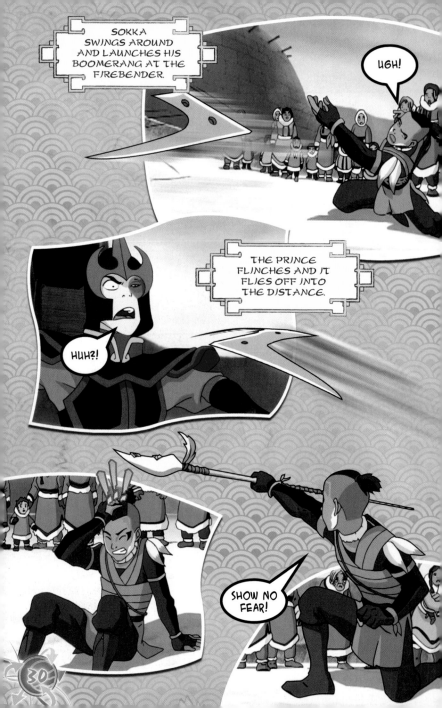

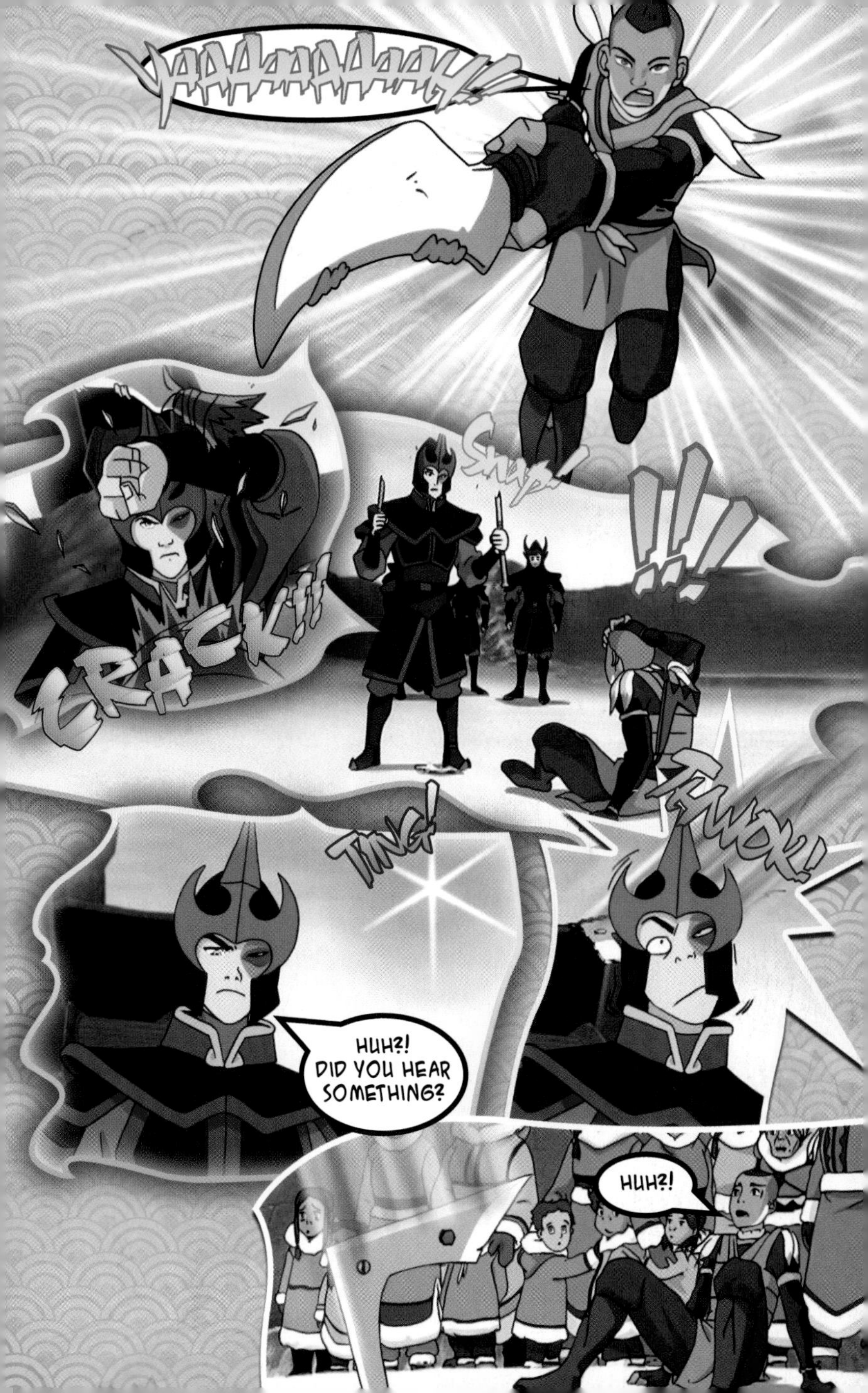
YAAAAAAAAAH!!
SNAP!
!!!
CRACK!!!
TING!
THWOK!
HUH?! DID YOU HEAR SOMETHING?
HUH?!

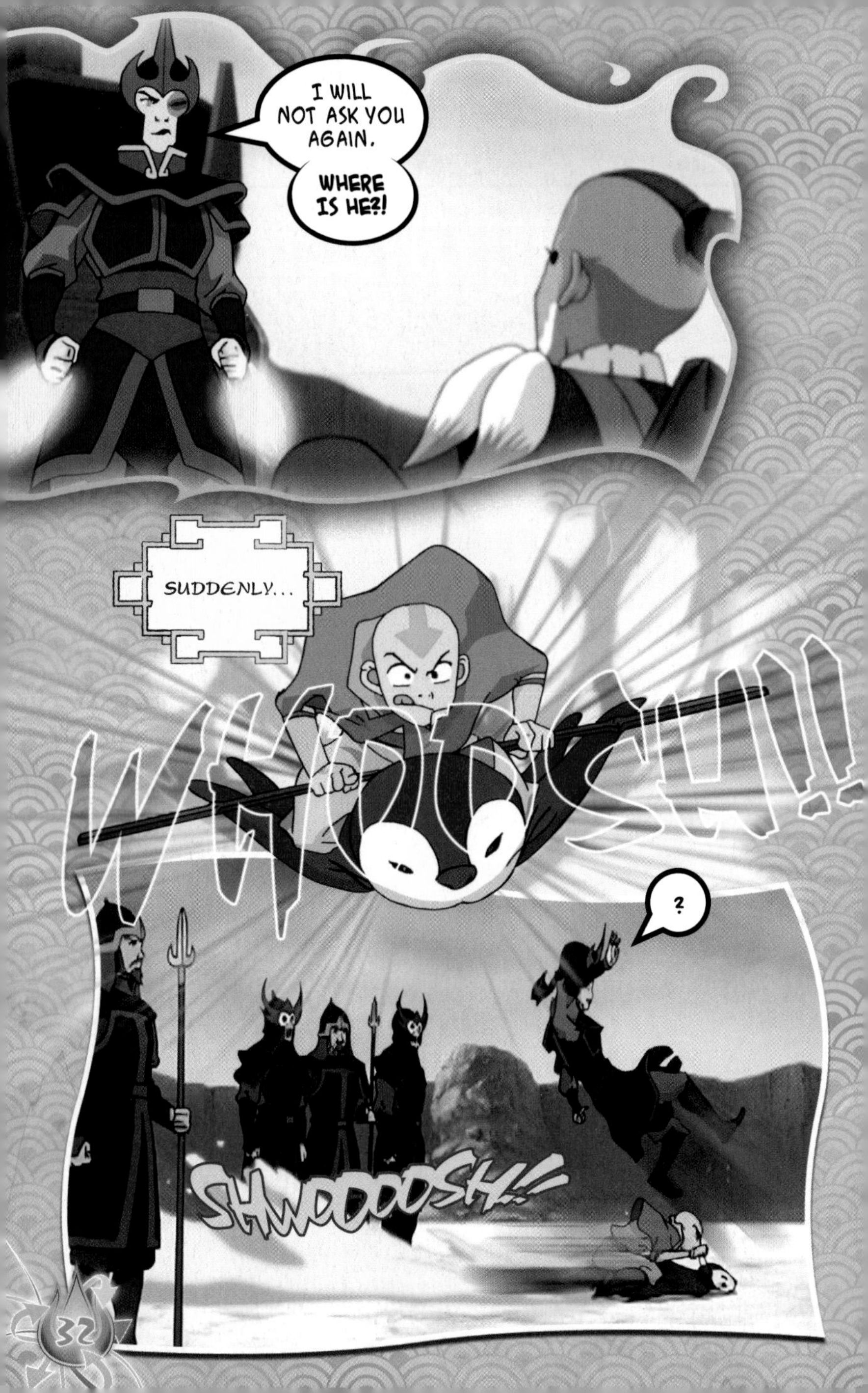
I WILL NOT ASK YOU AGAIN.
WHERE IS HE?!
SUDDENLY...
WHOOSH!!
?
SHWOOOOSH!!

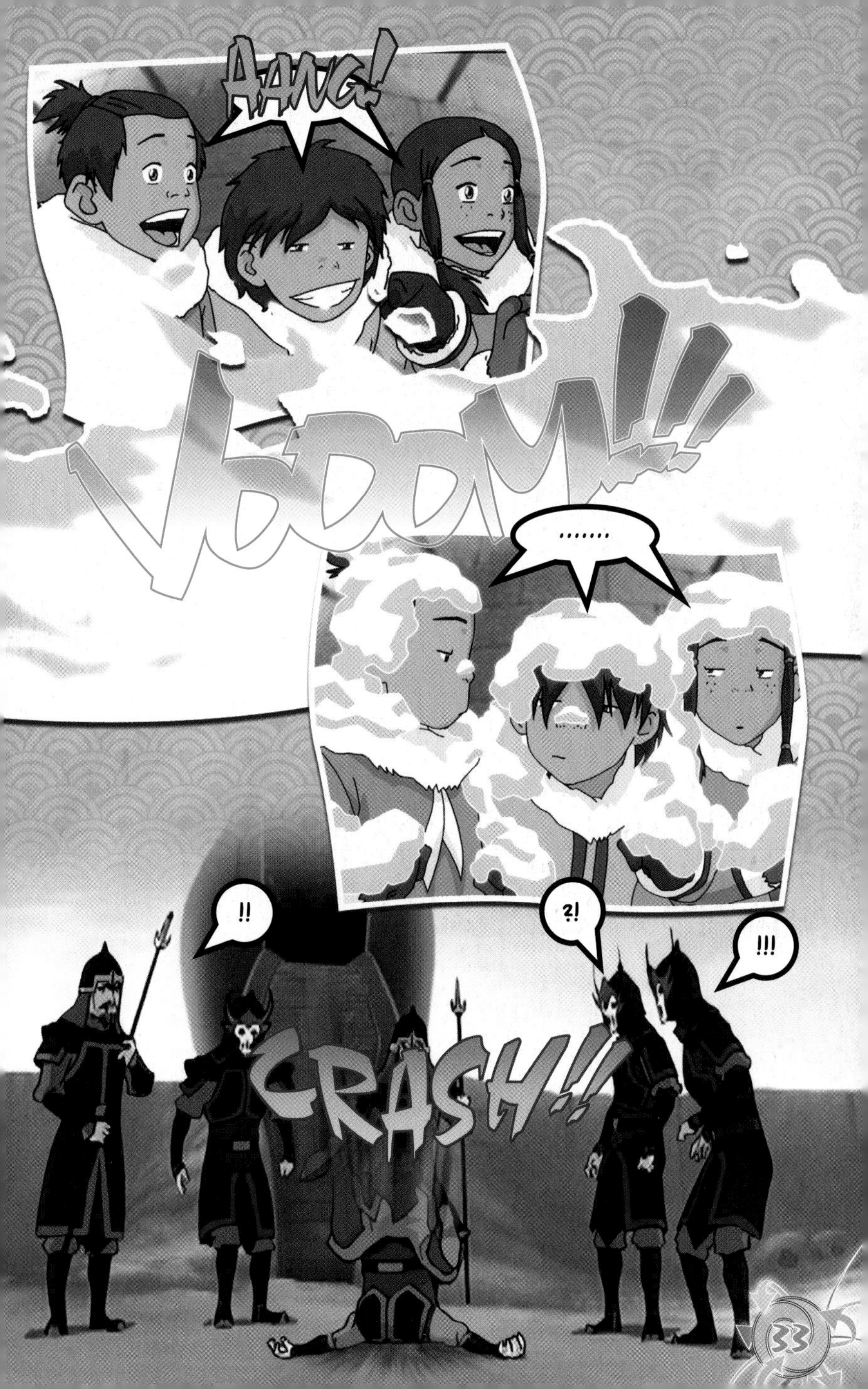
AANG!
VOOOM!!!
....
!!
?!
!!!
CRASH!!

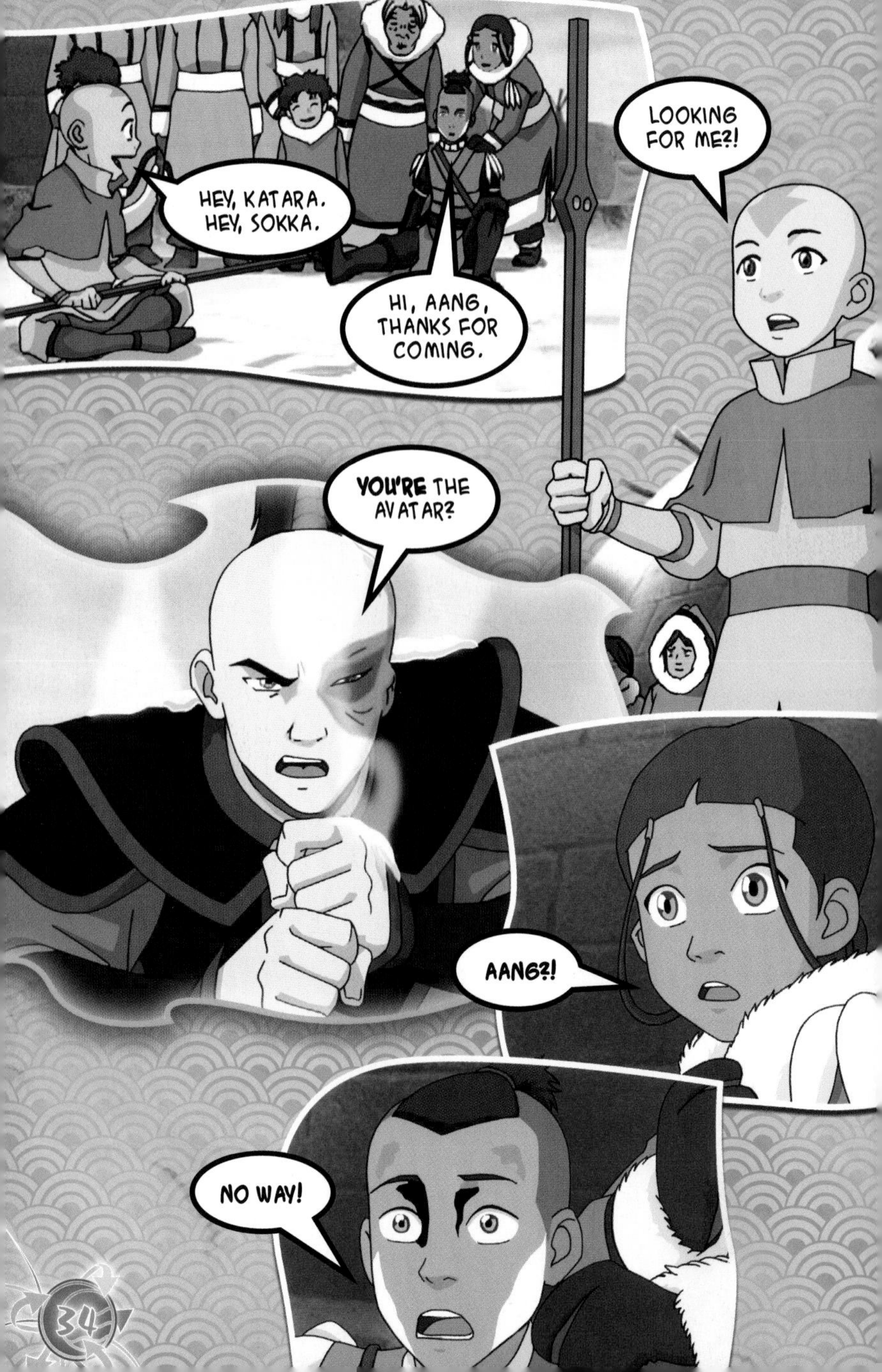
HEY, KATARA. HEY, SOKKA.
HI, AANG, THANKS FOR COMING.
LOOKING FOR ME?!
YOU'RE THE AVATAR?
AANG?!
NO WAY!

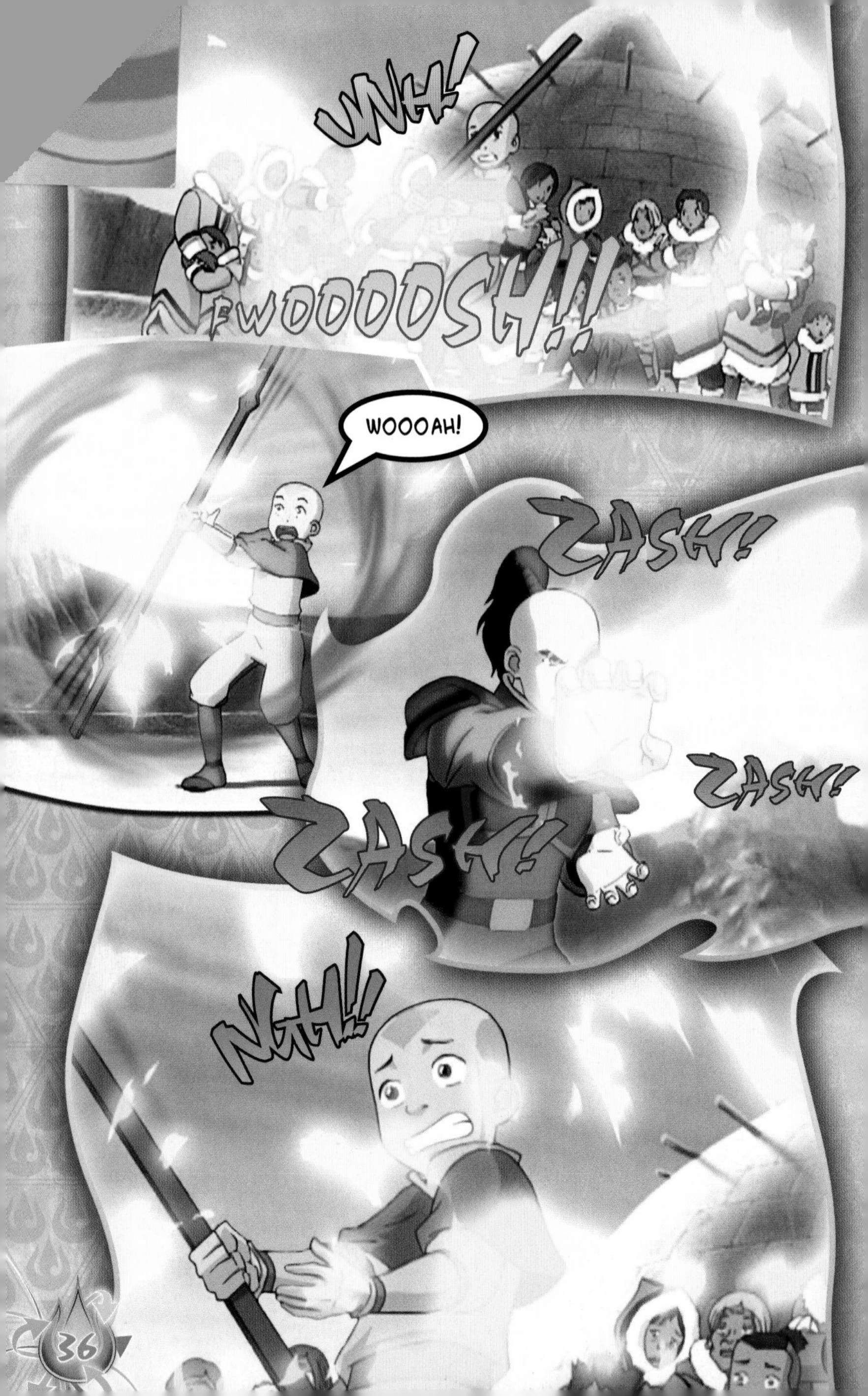
UNH!
FWOOOOSH!!
WOOOAH!
ZASH!
ZASH!
ZASH!
NGH!!

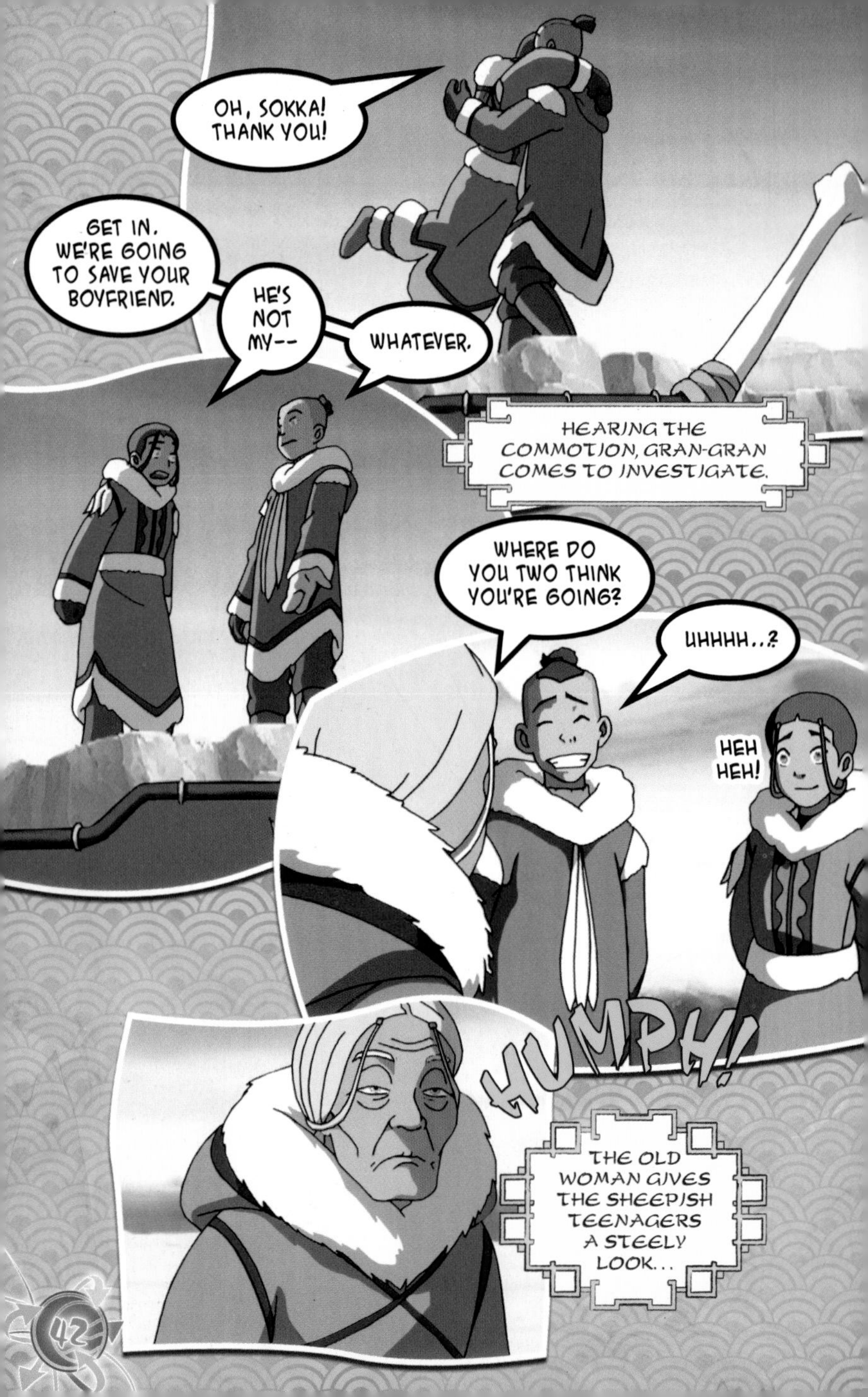
OH, SOKKA! THANK YOU!
GET IN. WE'RE GOING TO SAVE YOUR BOYFRIEND.
HE'S NOT MY--
WHATEVER.
HEARING THE COMMOTION, GRAN-GRAN COMES TO INVESTIGATE.
WHERE DO YOU TWO THINK YOU'RE GOING?
UHHHH...?
HEH HEH!
HUMPH!
THE OLD WOMAN GIVES THE SHEEPISH TEENAGERS A STEELY LOOK...
42

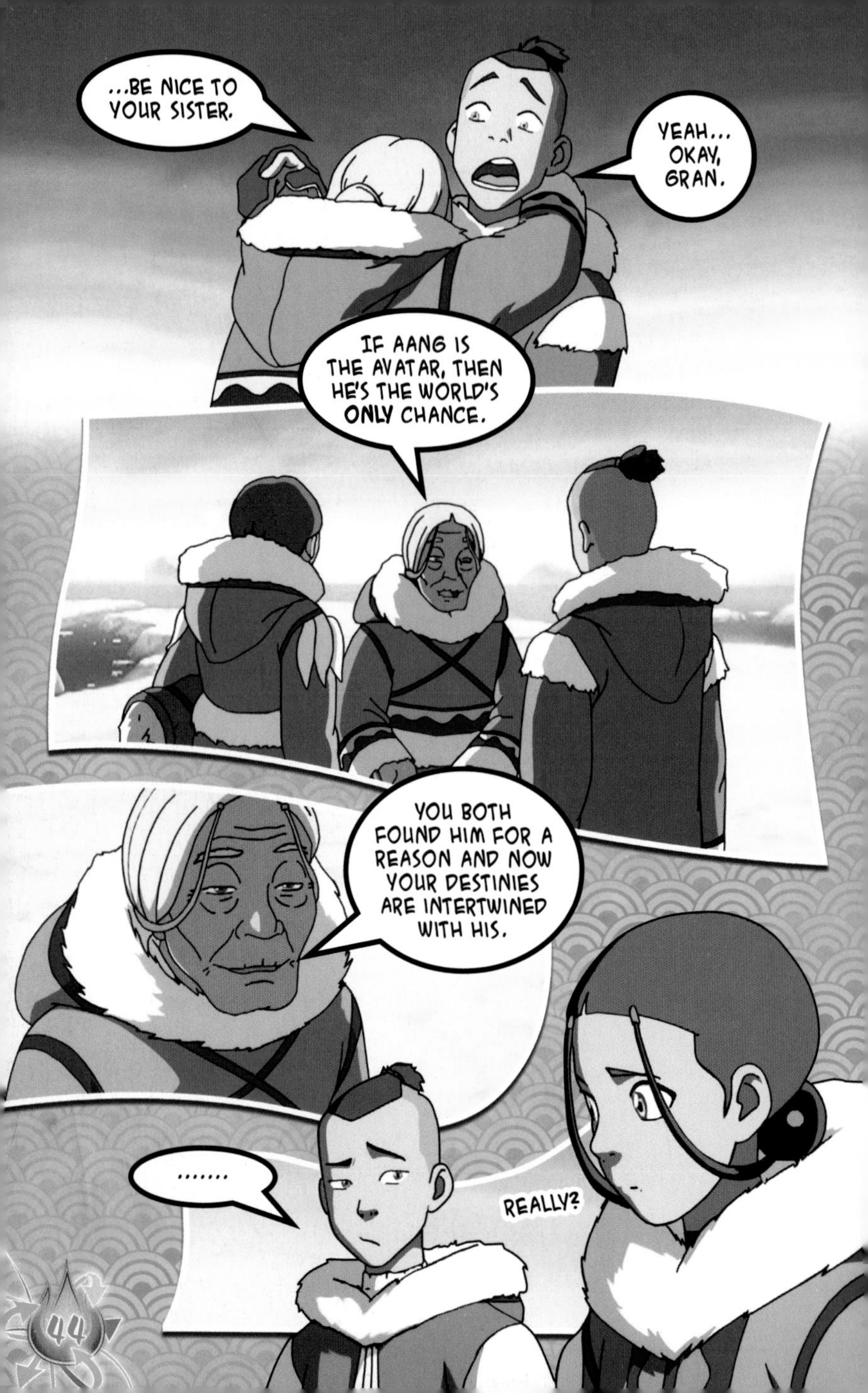
...BE NICE TO YOUR SISTER.
YEAH... OKAY, GRAN.
IF AANG IS THE AVATAR, THEN HE'S THE WORLD'S ONLY CHANCE.
YOU BOTH FOUND HIM FOR A REASON AND NOW YOUR DESTINIES ARE INTERTWINED WITH HIS.
....
REALLY?

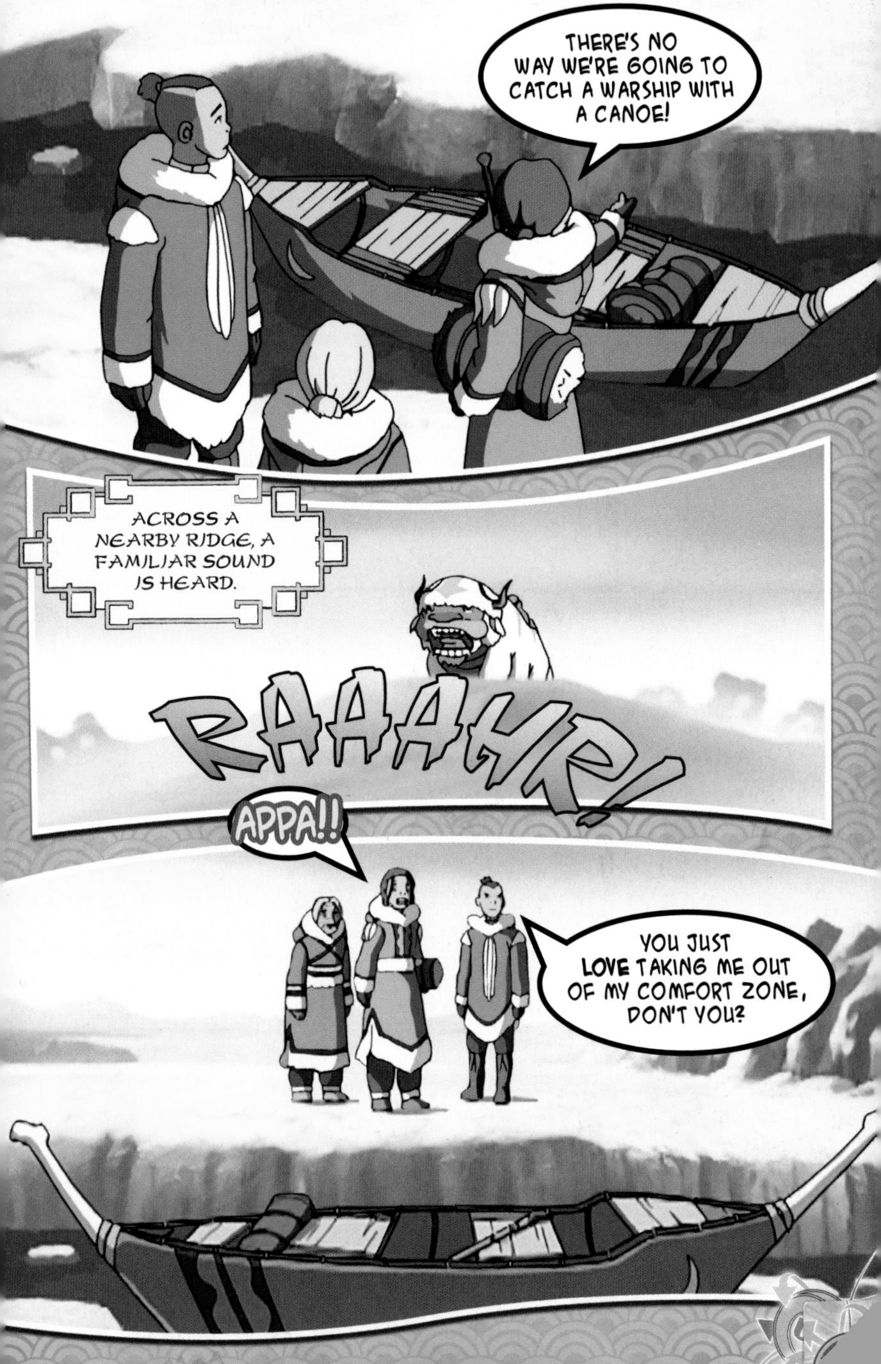
THERE'S NO WAY WE'RE GOING TO CATCH A WARSHIP WITH A CANOE!
ACROSS A NEARBY RIDGE, A FAMILIAR SOUND IS HEARD.
RAAAHR!
APPA!!
YOU JUST LOVE TAKING ME OUT OF MY COMFORT ZONE, DON'T YOU?

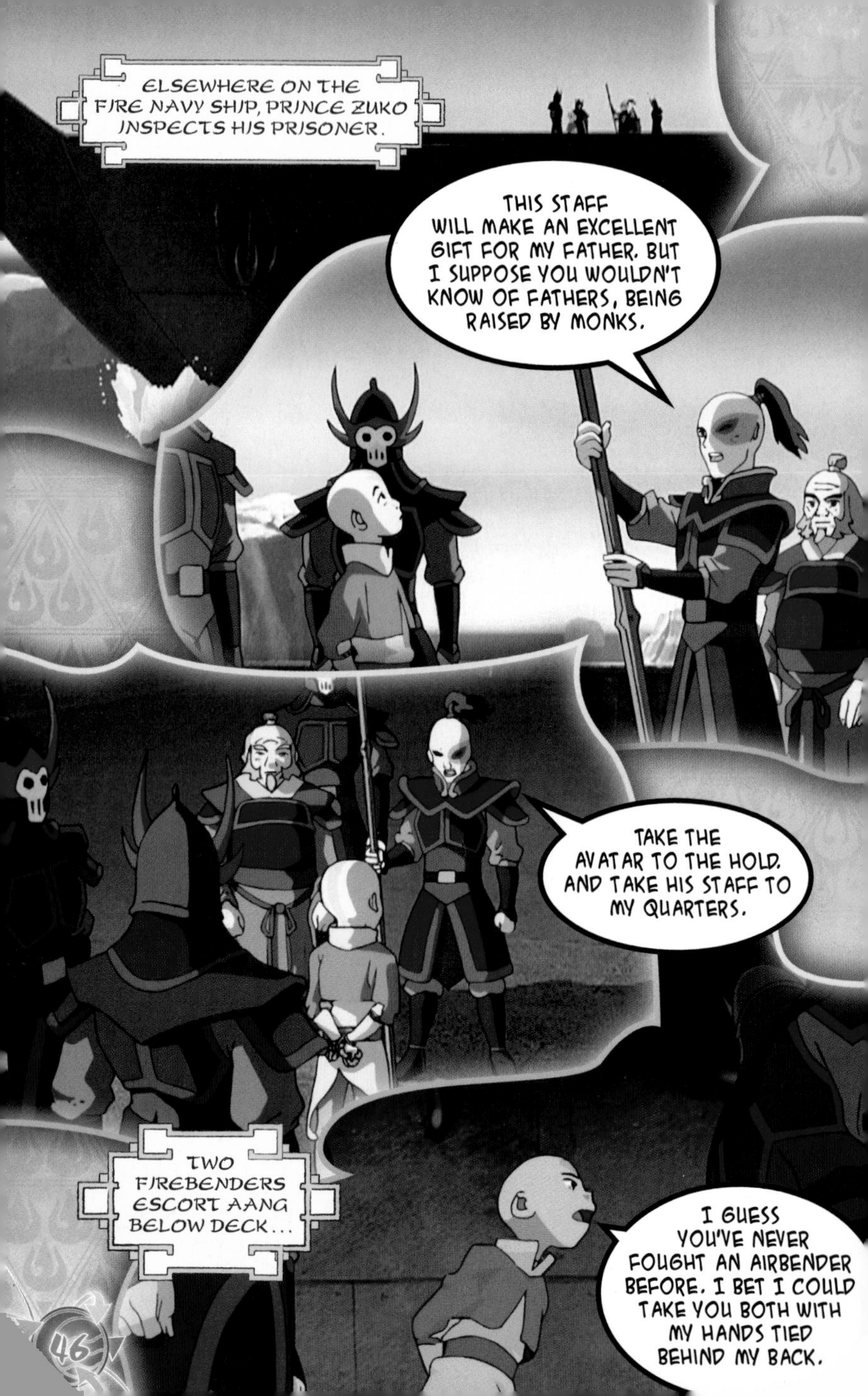
ELSEWHERE ON THE FIRE NAVY SHIP, PRINCE ZUKO INSPECTS HIS PRISONER.
THIS STAFF WILL MAKE AN EXCELLENT GIFT FOR MY FATHER. BUT I SUPPOSE YOU WOULDN'T KNOW OF FATHERS, BEING RAISED BY MONKS.
TAKE THE AVATAR TO THE HOLD. AND TAKE HIS STAFF TO MY QUARTERS.
TWO FIREBENDERS ESCORT AANG BELOW DECK...
I GUESS YOU'VE NEVER FOUGHT AN AIRBENDER BEFORE. I BET I COULD TAKE YOU BOTH WITH MY HANDS TIED BEHIND MY BACK.

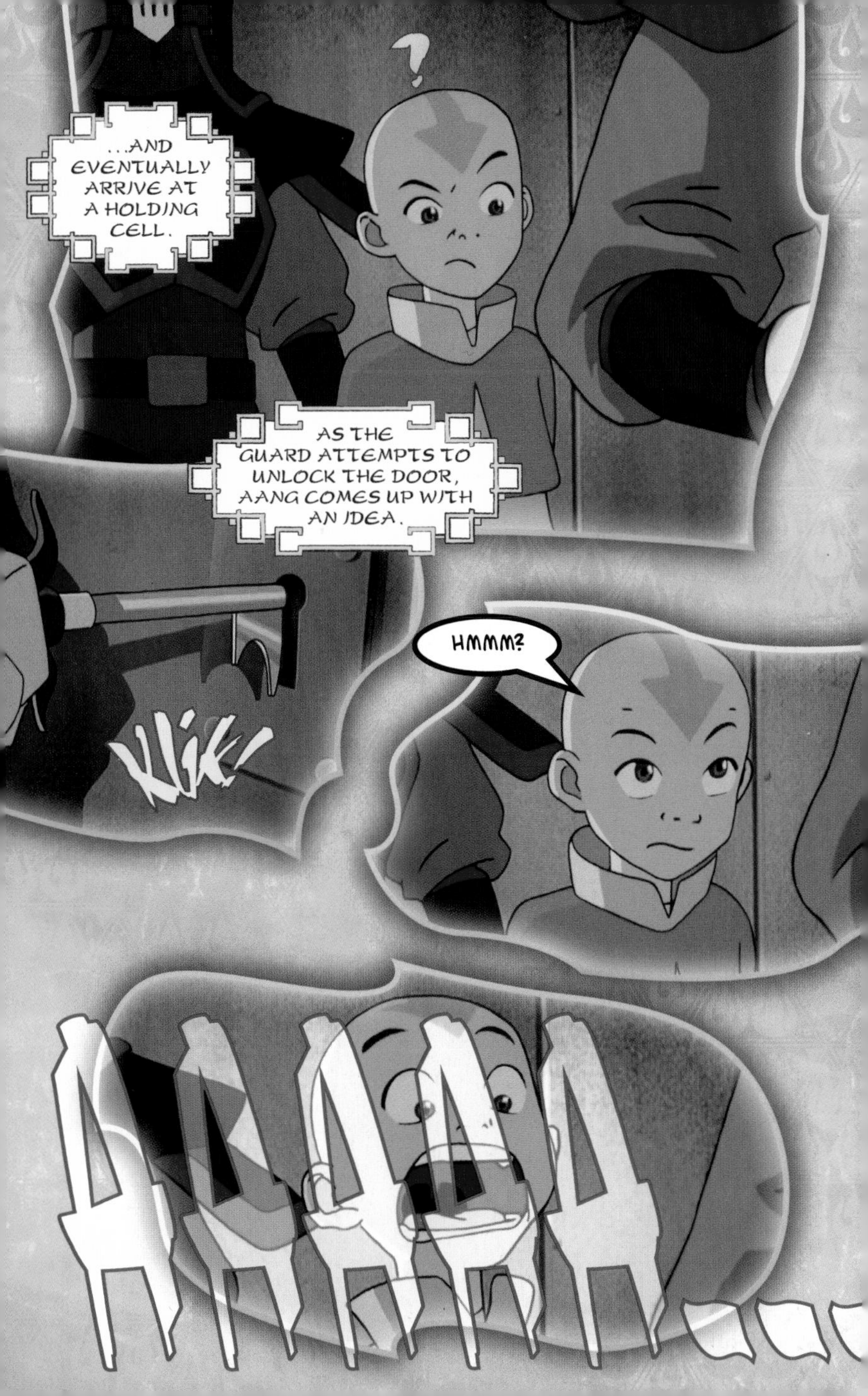

...AND EVENTUALLY ARRIVE AT A HOLDING CELL.
?
AS THE GUARD ATTEMPTS TO UNLOCK THE DOOR, AANG COMES UP WITH AN IDEA.
KLIK!
HMMM?
AAAAA...

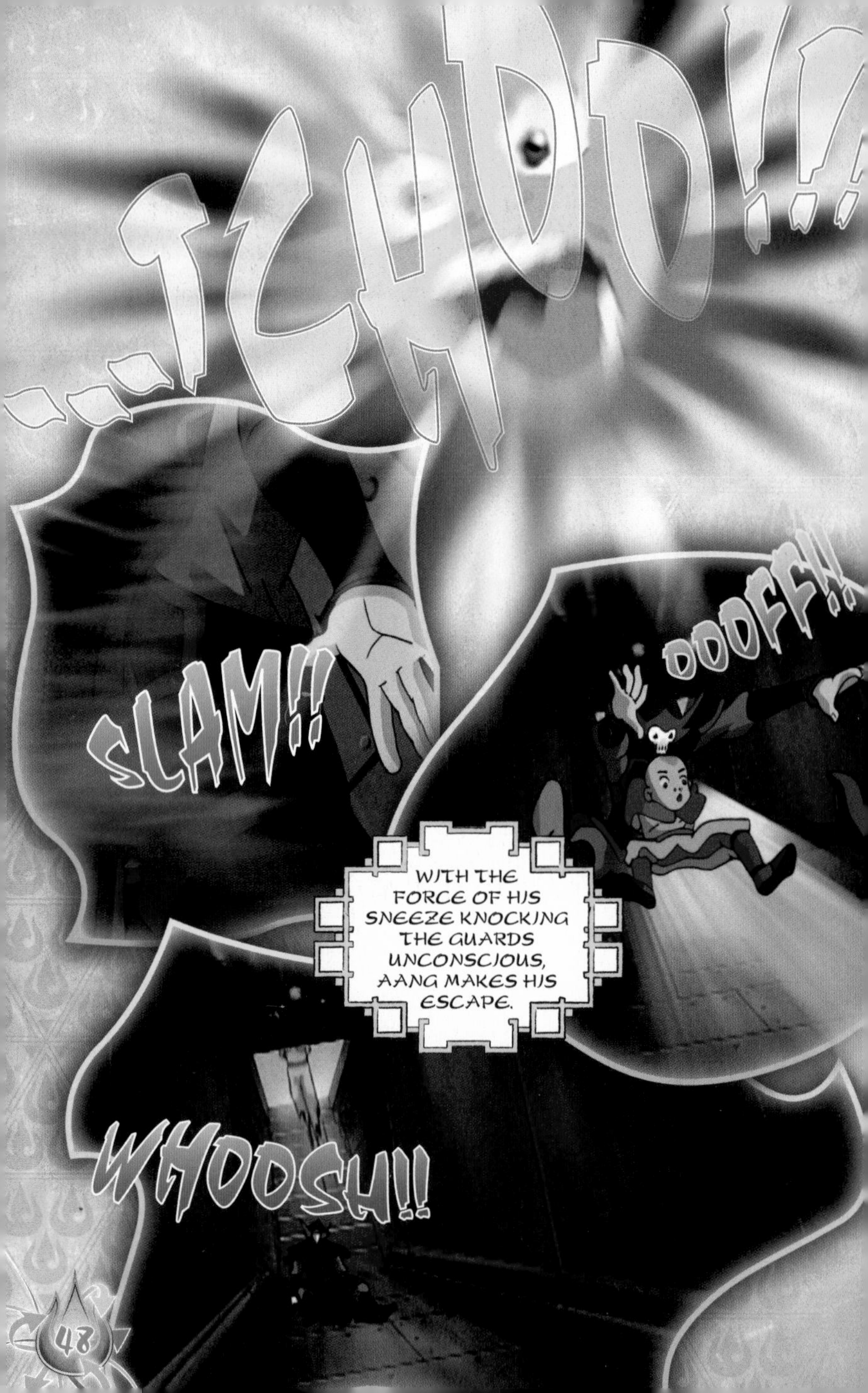
...ICHOO!!!
SLAM!!
OOOFF!!
WITH THE FORCE OF HIS SNEEZE KNOCKING THE GUARDS UNCONSCIOUS, AANG MAKES HIS ESCAPE.
WHOOSH!!

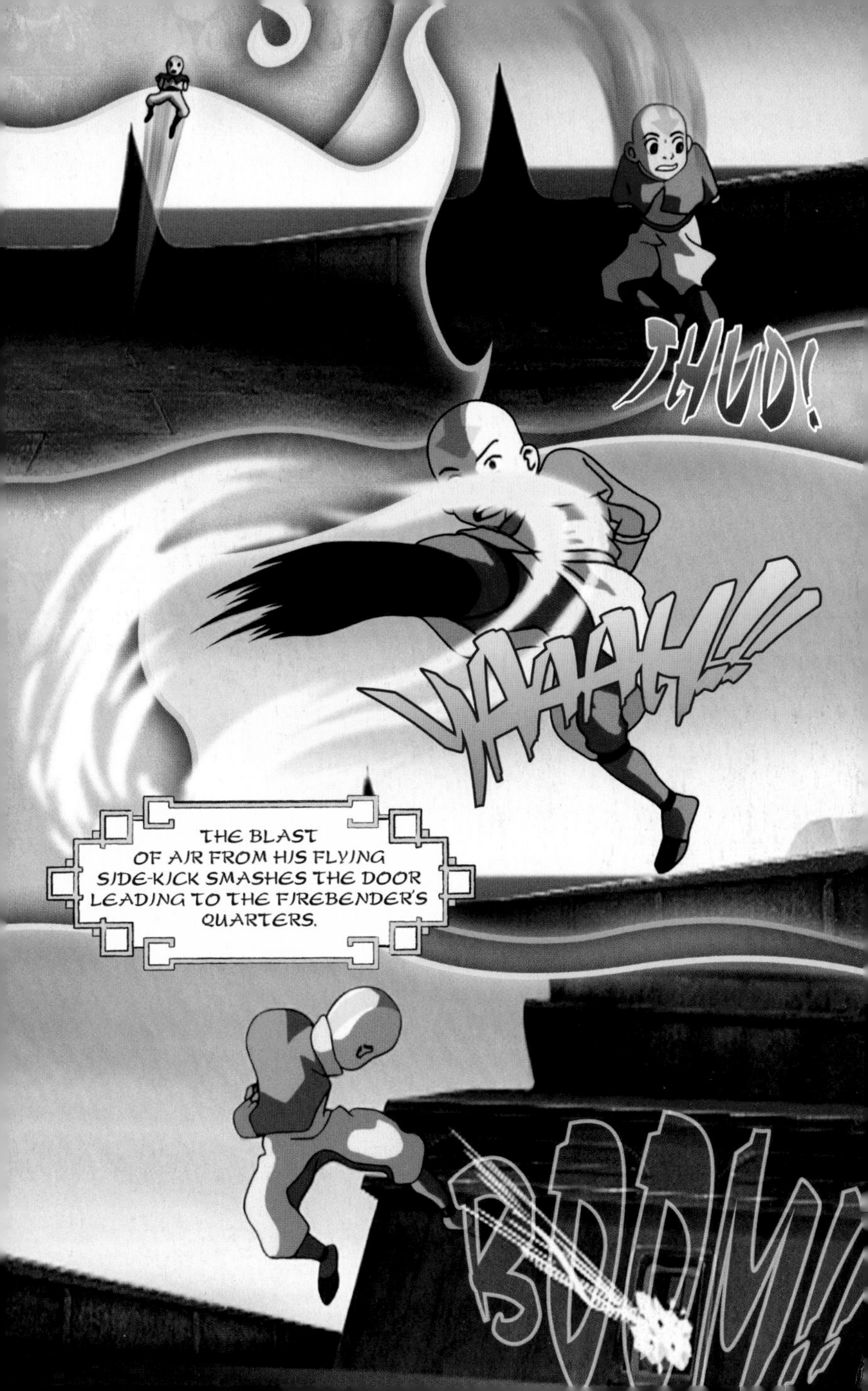
THUD!
WAAAH!!
THE BLAST OF AIR FROM HIS FLYING SIDE-KICK SMASHES THE DOOR LEADING TO THE FIREBENDER'S QUARTERS.
BOOM!!

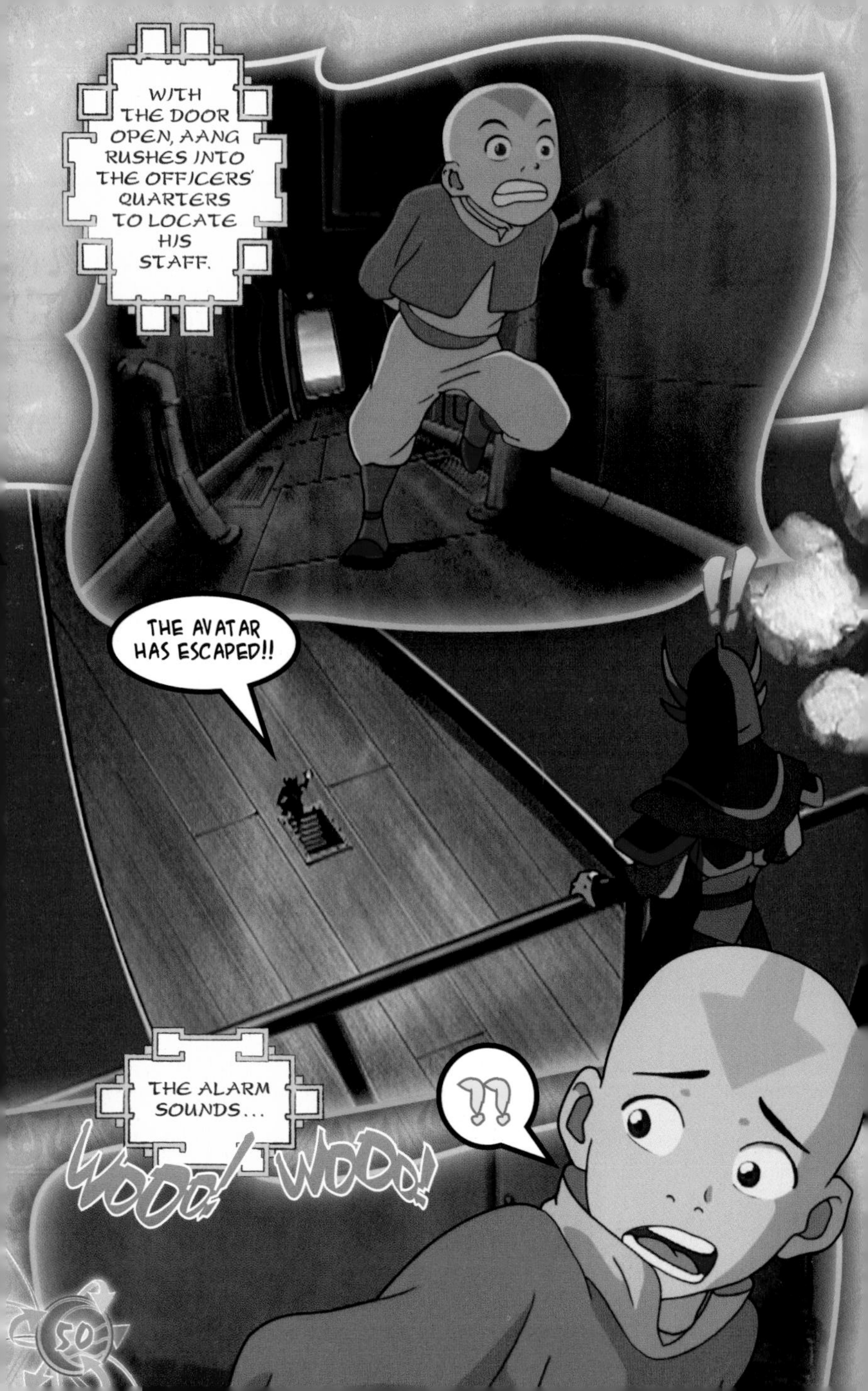
WITH THE DOOR OPEN, AANG RUSHES INTO THE OFFICERS' QUARTERS TO LOCATE HIS STAFF.
THE AVATAR HAS ESCAPED!!
THE ALARM SOUNDS...
WOOO! WOOO!
!!

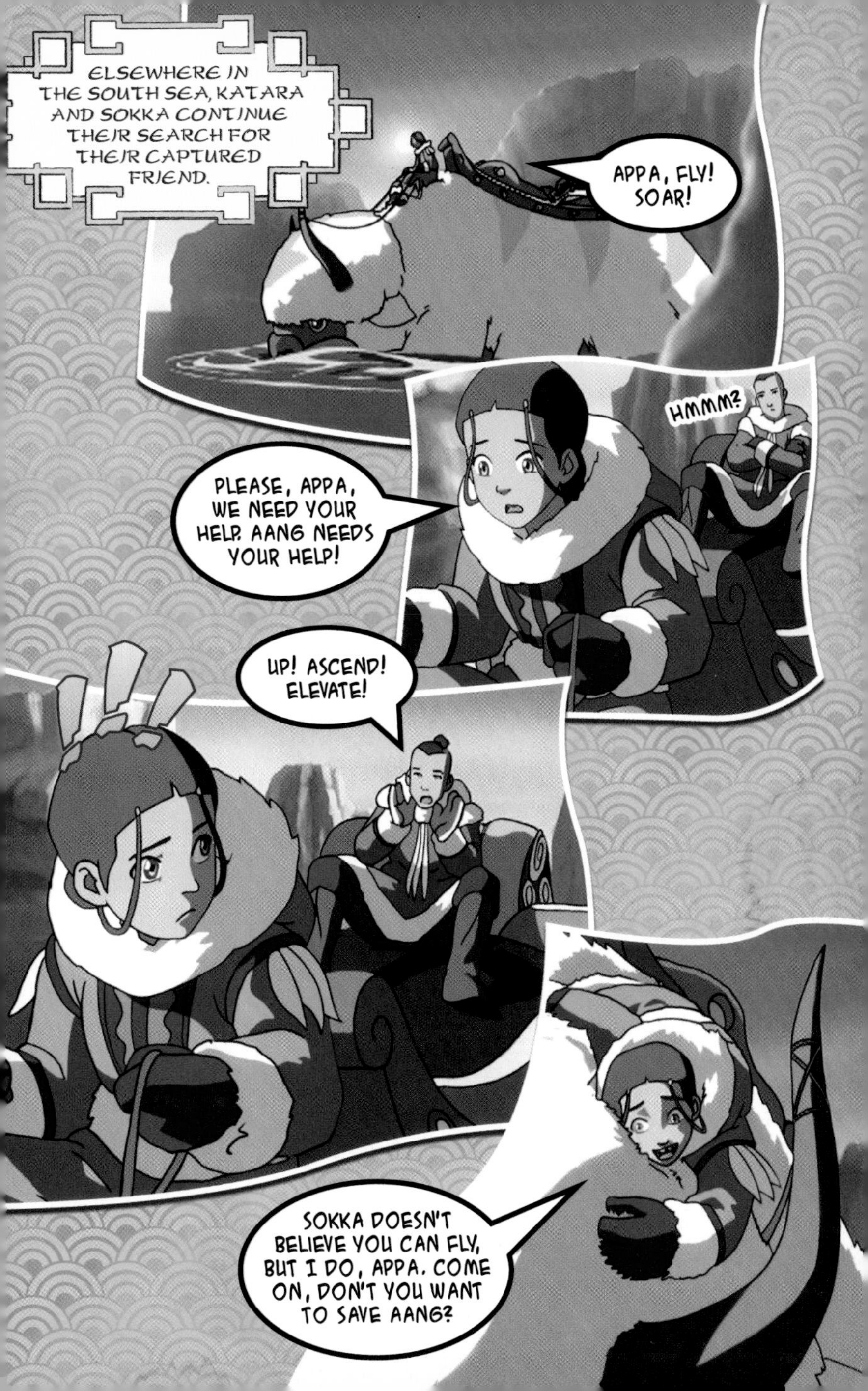
ELSEWHERE IN THE SOUTH SEA, KATARA AND SOKKA CONTINUE THEIR SEARCH FOR THEIR CAPTURED FRIEND.
APPA, FLY! SOAR!
PLEASE, APPA, WE NEED YOUR HELP. AANG NEEDS YOUR HELP!
HMMM?
UP! ASCEND! ELEVATE!
SOKKA DOESN'T BELIEVE YOU CAN FLY, BUT I DO, APPA. COME ON, DON'T YOU WANT TO SAVE AANG?

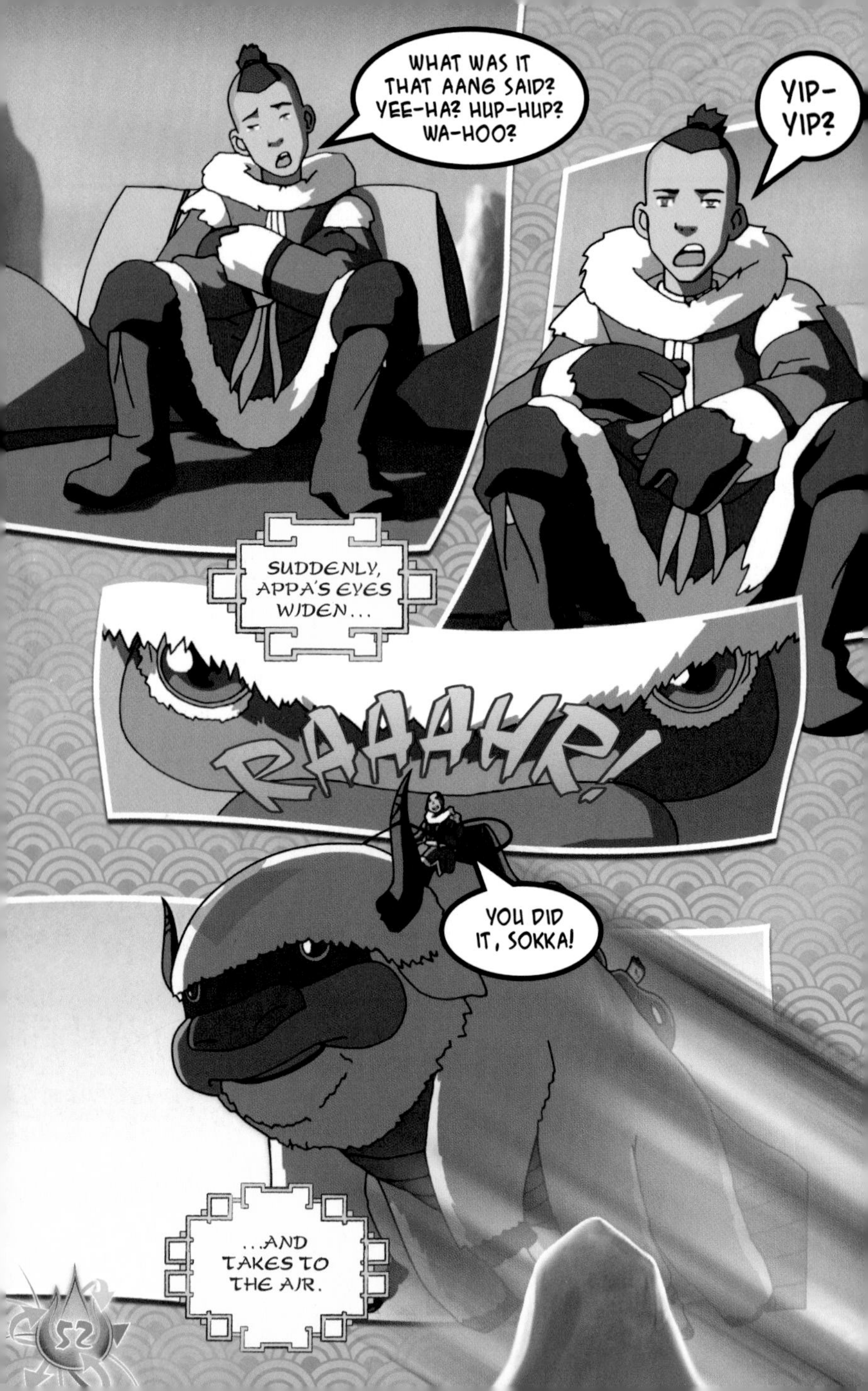
WHAT WAS IT THAT AANG SAID? YEE-HA? HUP-HUP? WA-HOO?
YIP-YIP?
SUDDENLY, APPA'S EYES WIDEN...
RAAAHR!
YOU DID IT, SOKKA!
...AND TAKES TO THE AIR.

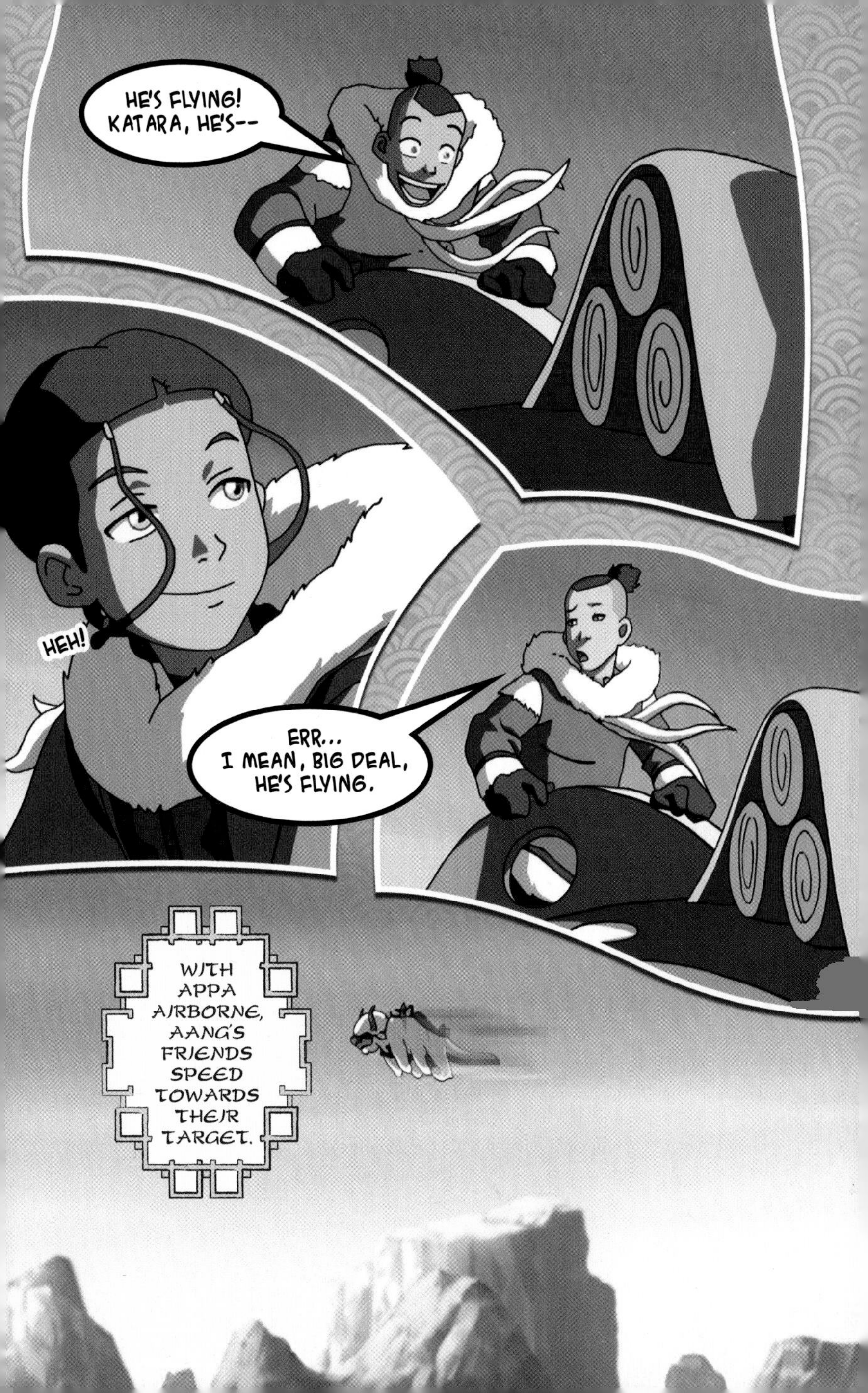
HE'S FLYING! KATARA, HE'S--
HEH!
ERR... I MEAN, BIG DEAL, HE'S FLYING.
WITH APPA AIRBORNE, AANG'S FRIENDS SPEED TOWARDS THEIR TARGET.

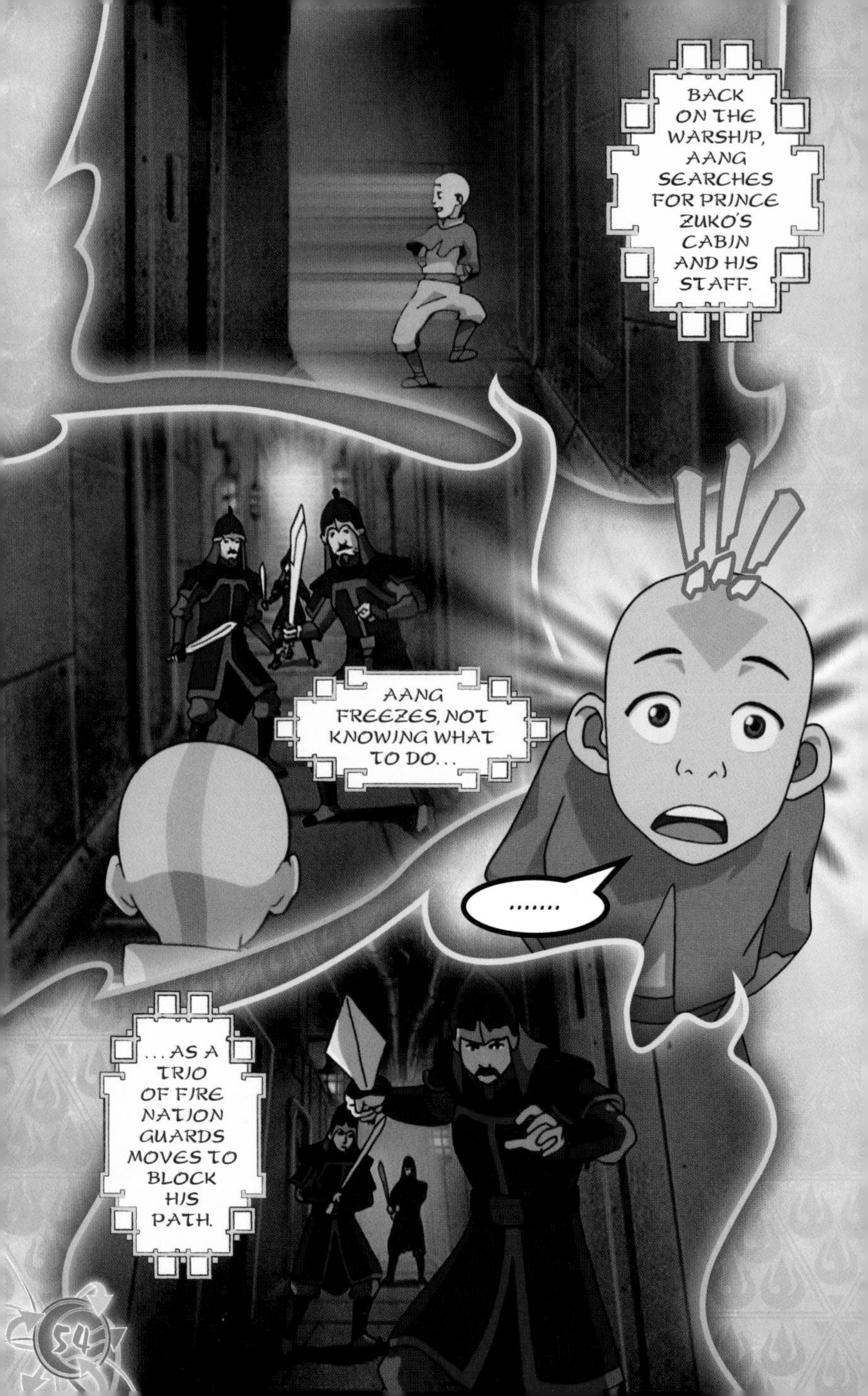
BACK ON THE WARSHIP, AANG SEARCHES FOR PRINCE ZUKO'S CABIN AND HIS STAFF.
AANG FREEZES, NOT KNOWING WHAT TO DO...
....
...AS A TRIO OF FIRE NATION GUARDS MOVES TO BLOCK HIS PATH.

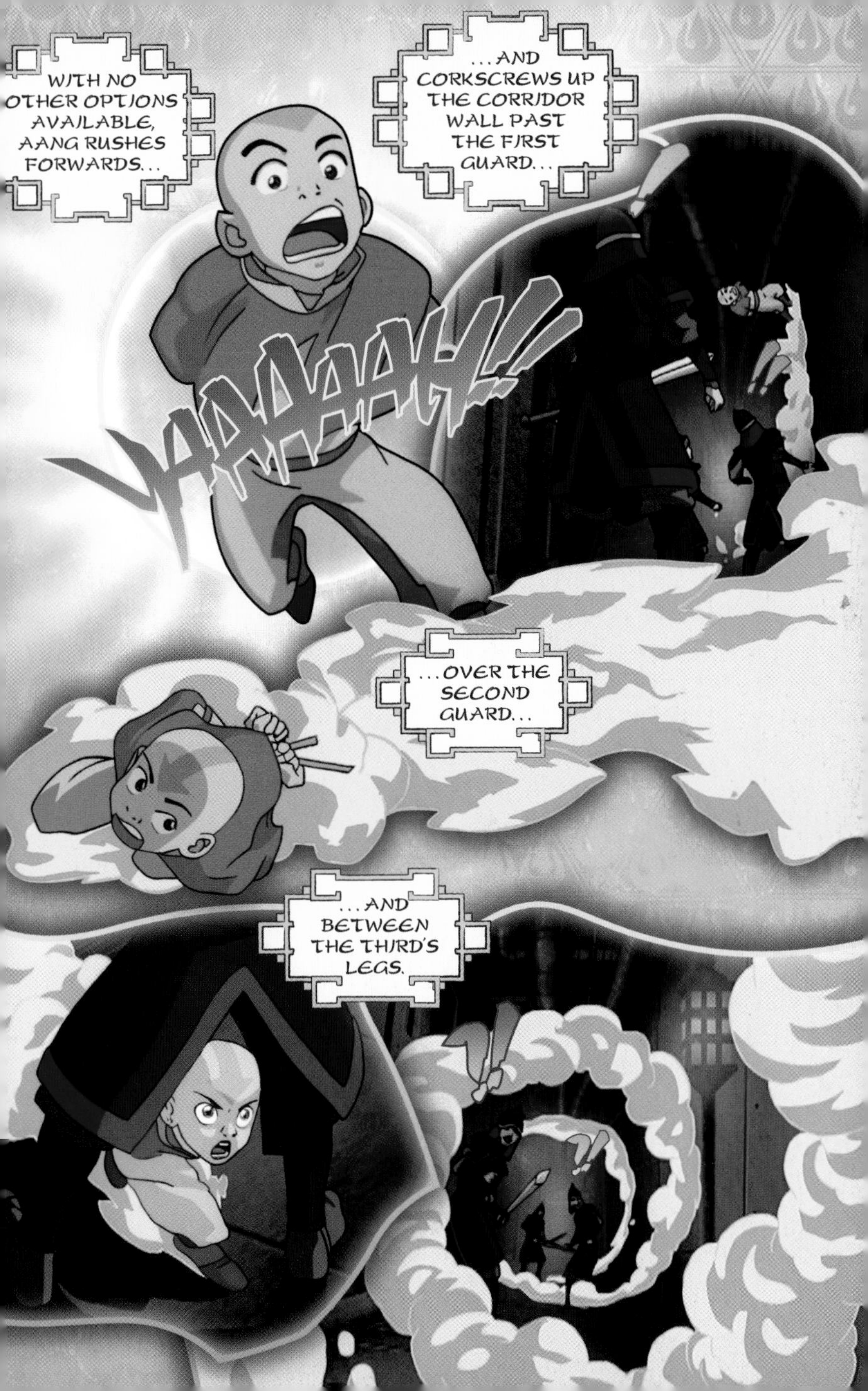
WITH NO OTHER OPTIONS AVAILABLE, AANG RUSHES FORWARDS...
...AND CORKSCREWS UP THE CORRIDOR WALL PAST THE FIRST GUARD...
YAAAAAH!!
...OVER THE SECOND GUARD...
...AND BETWEEN THE THIRD'S LEGS.

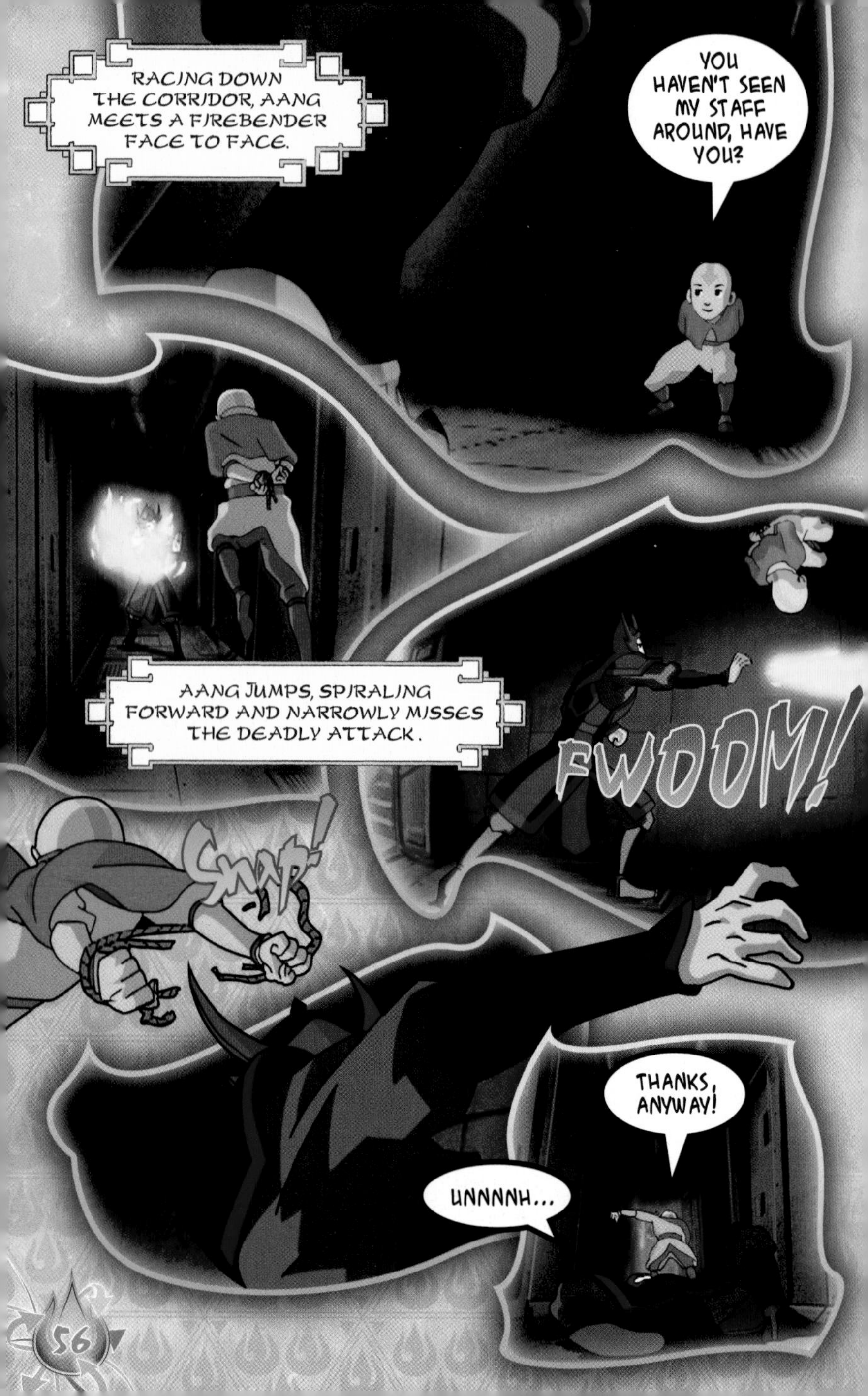
RACING DOWN THE CORRIDOR, AANG MEETS A FIREBENDER FACE TO FACE.
YOU HAVEN'T SEEN MY STAFF AROUND, HAVE YOU?
AANG JUMPS, SPIRALING FORWARD AND NARROWLY MISSES THE DEADLY ATTACK.
FWOOM!
SNAP!
THANKS, ANYWAY!
UNNNNH...

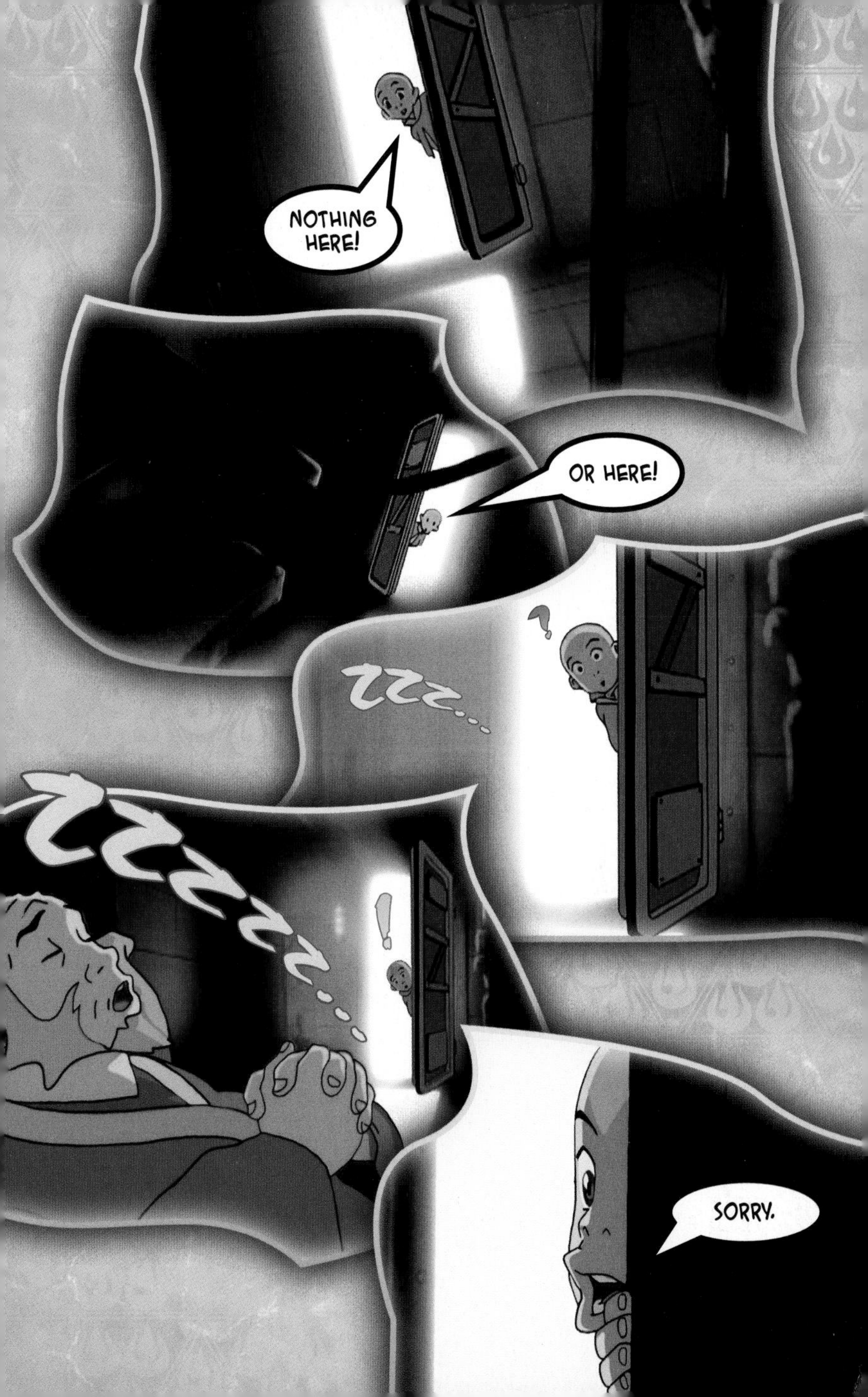
NOTHING HERE!
OR HERE!
ZZZ...
ZZZZZ....
SORRY.

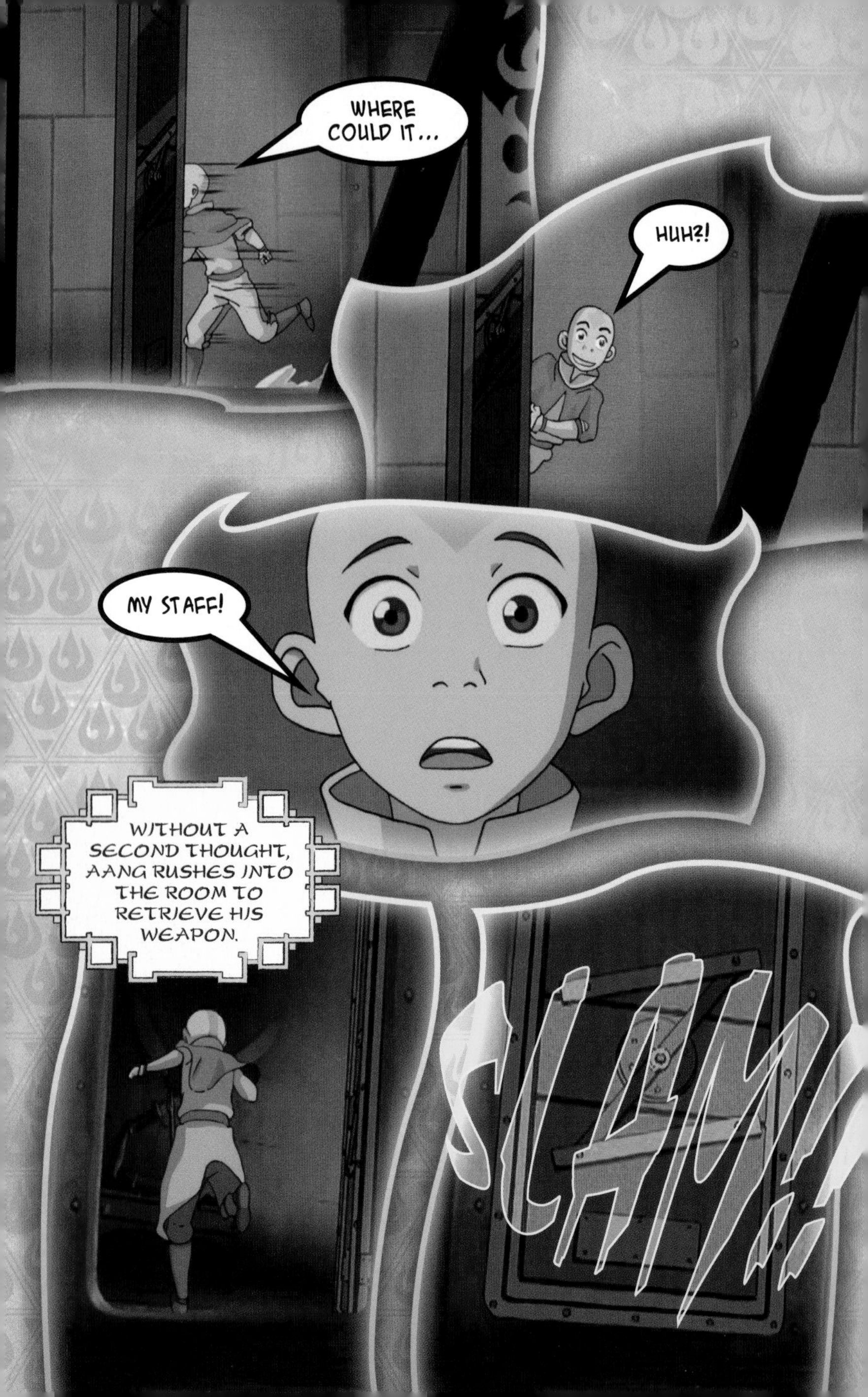
WHERE COULD IT...
HUH?!
MY STAFF!
WITHOUT A SECOND THOUGHT, AANG RUSHES INTO THE ROOM TO RETRIEVE HIS WEAPON.
SLAM!!

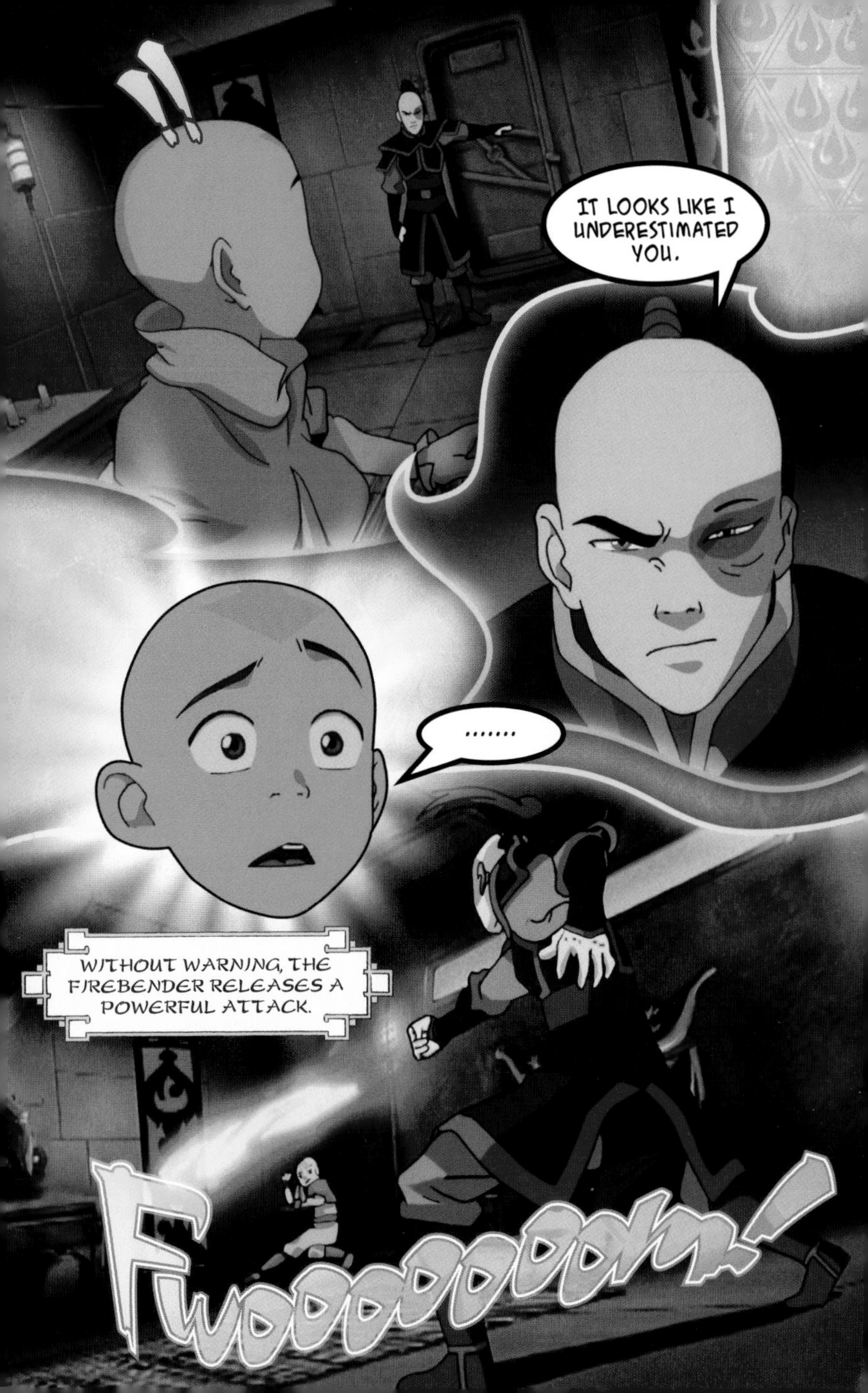

IT LOOKS LIKE I UNDERESTIMATED YOU.
....
WITHOUT WARNING, THE FIREBENDER RELEASES A POWERFUL ATTACK.
FWOOOOOOOM!

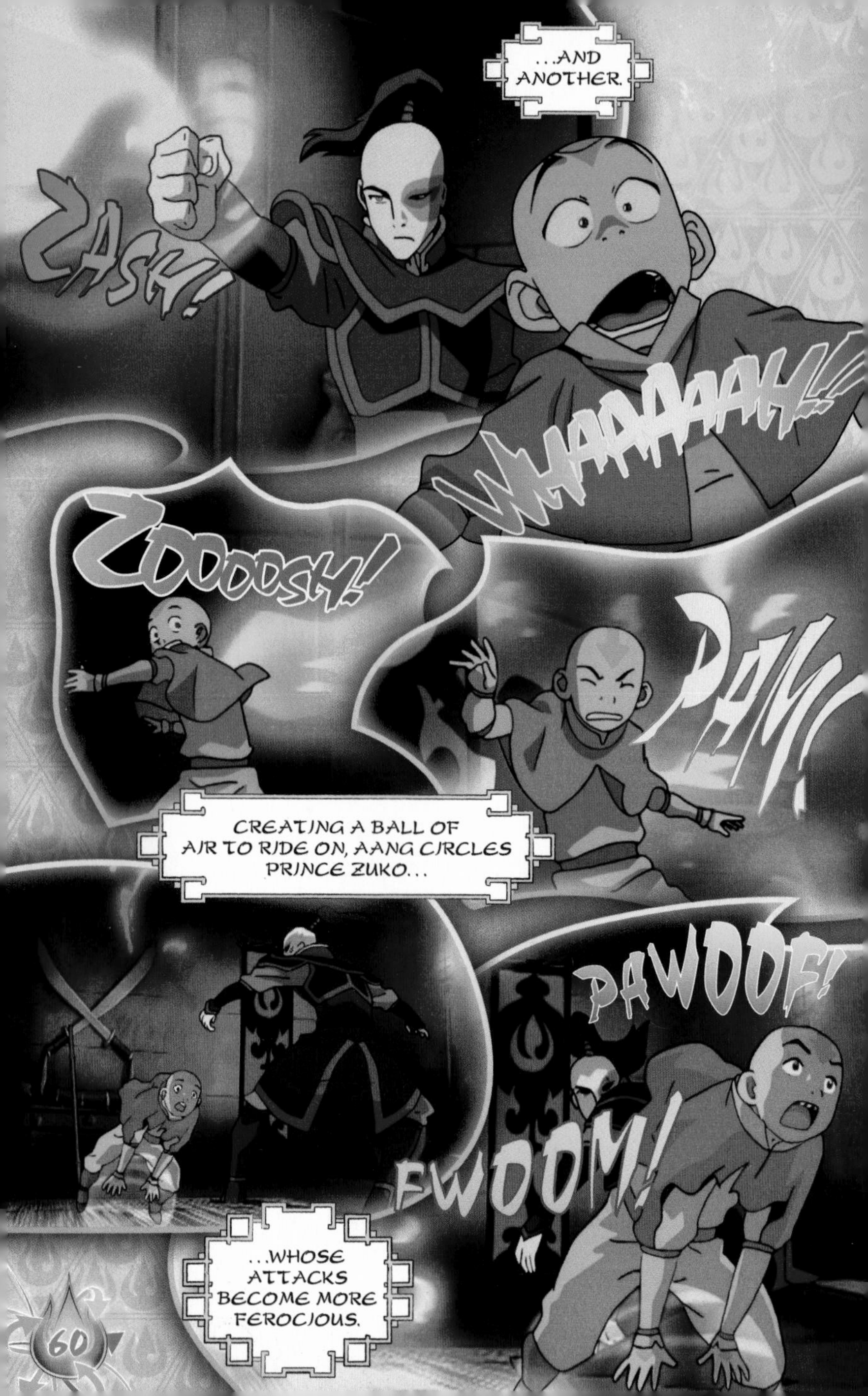
...AND ANOTHER.
ZASH!
WHAAAAAH!!
ZOOOOOSH!
PAM!
CREATING A BALL OF AIR TO RIDE ON, AANG CIRCLES PRINCE ZUKO...
PAWOOF!
FWOOM!
...WHOSE ATTACKS BECOME MORE FEROCIOUS.

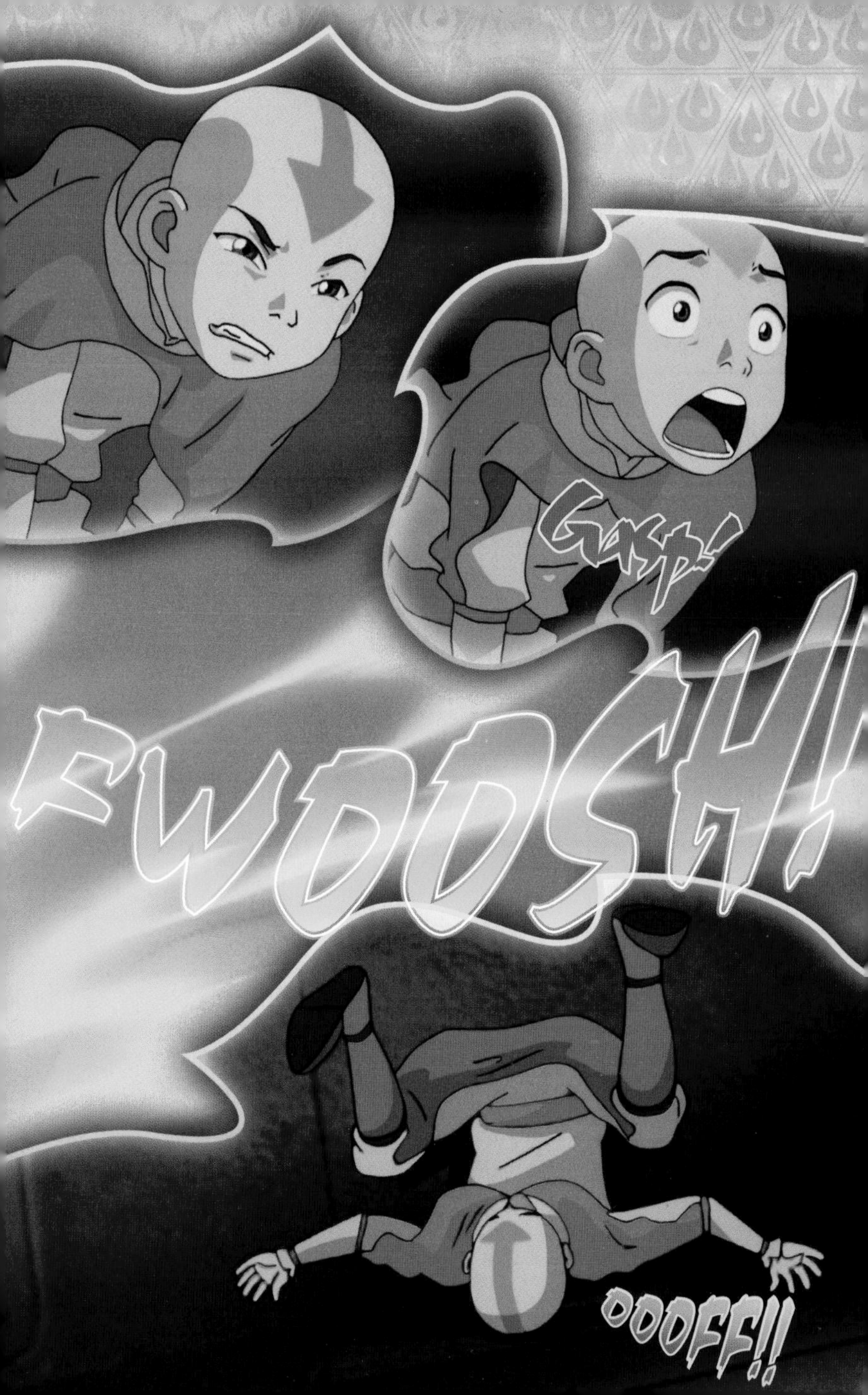
Gasp!
FWOOSH!
OOOFF!!

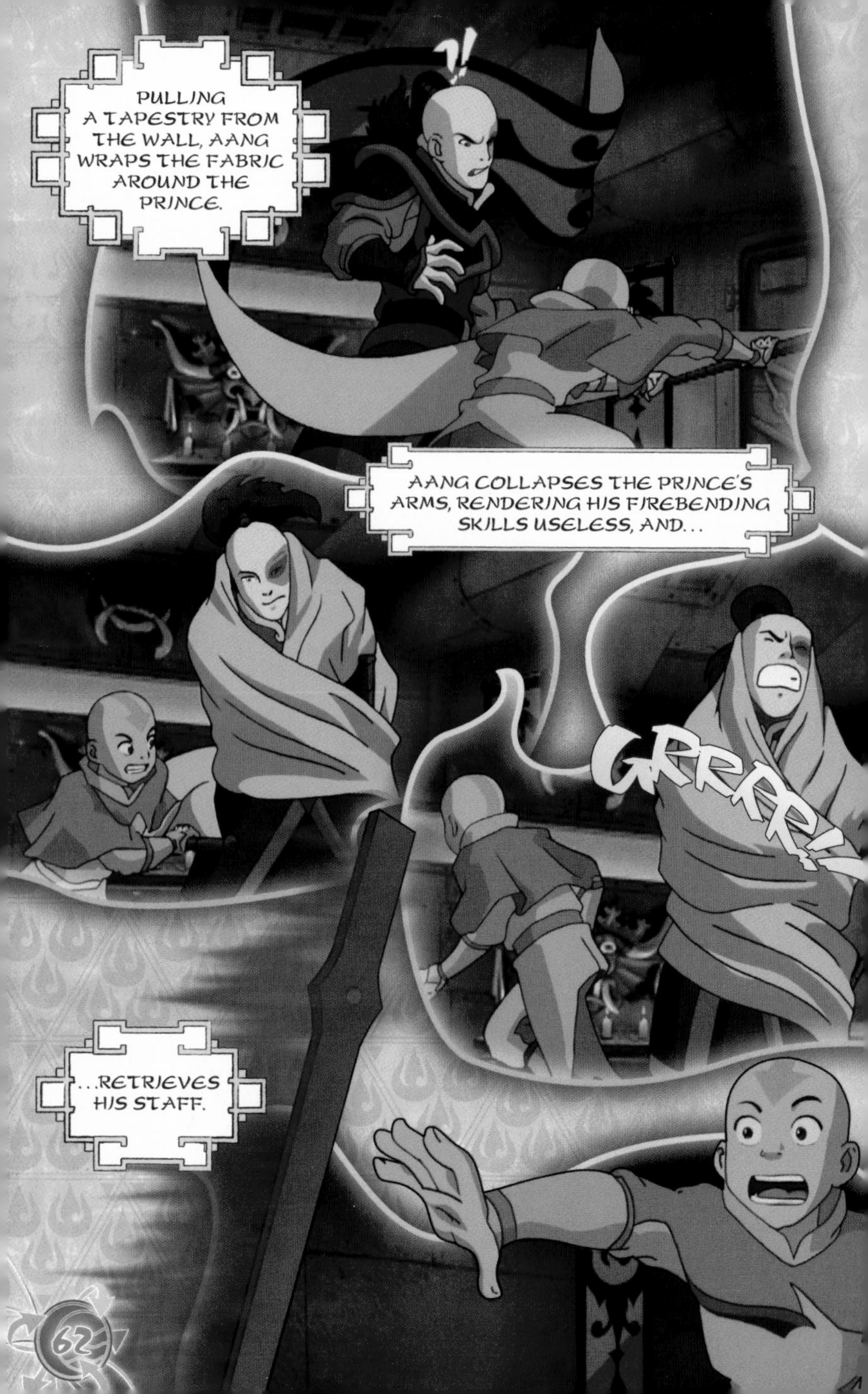
PULLING A TAPESTRY FROM THE WALL, AANG WRAPS THE FABRIC AROUND THE PRINCE.
?!
AANG COLLAPSES THE PRINCE'S ARMS, RENDERING HIS FIREBENDING SKILLS USELESS, AND...
GRRRR!
...RETRIEVES HIS STAFF.

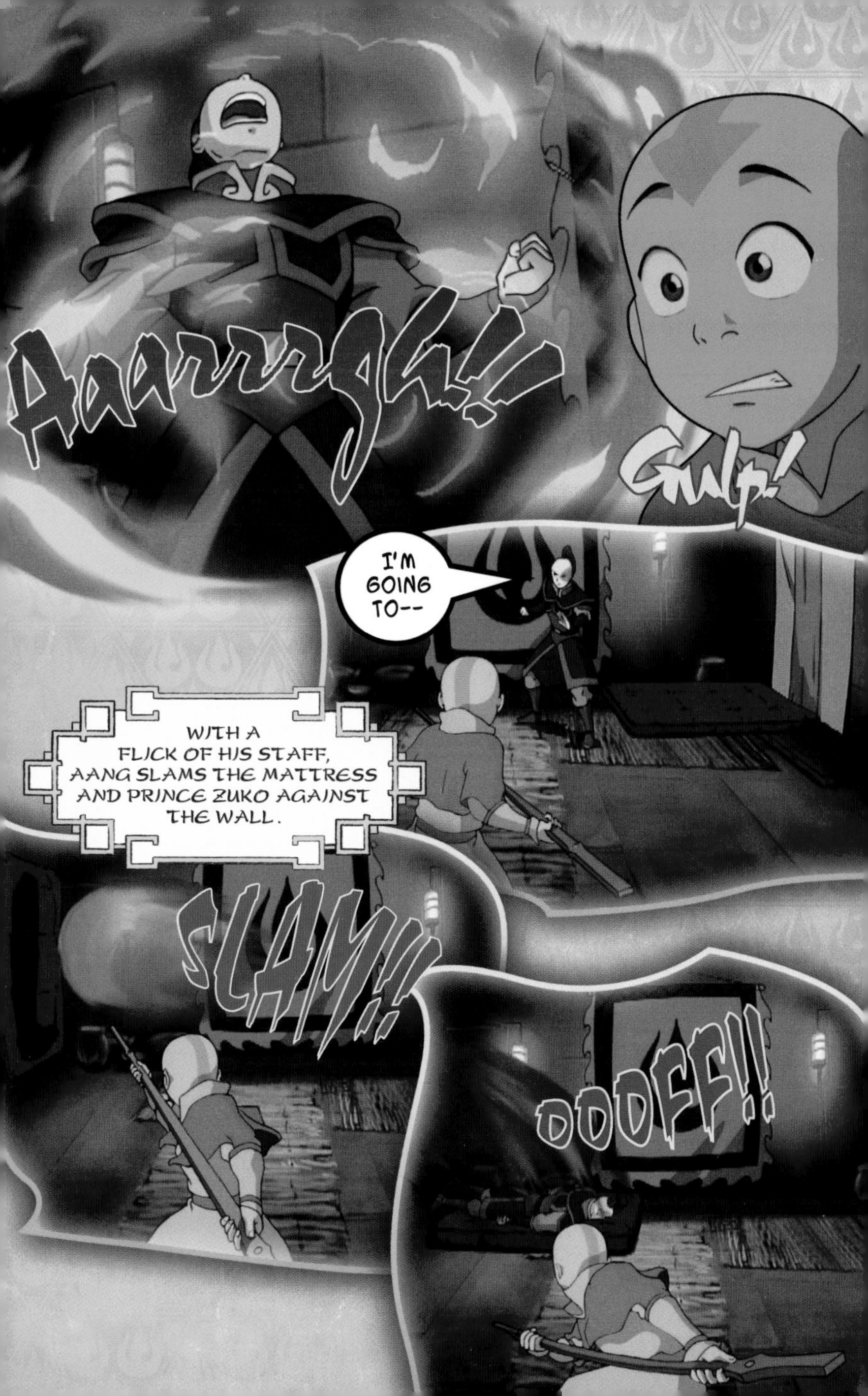
Aaarrrgh!!
Gulp!
I'M GOING TO--
WITH A FLICK OF HIS STAFF, AANG SLAMS THE MATTRESS AND PRINCE ZUKO AGAINST THE WALL.
SLAM!!
OOOFF!!

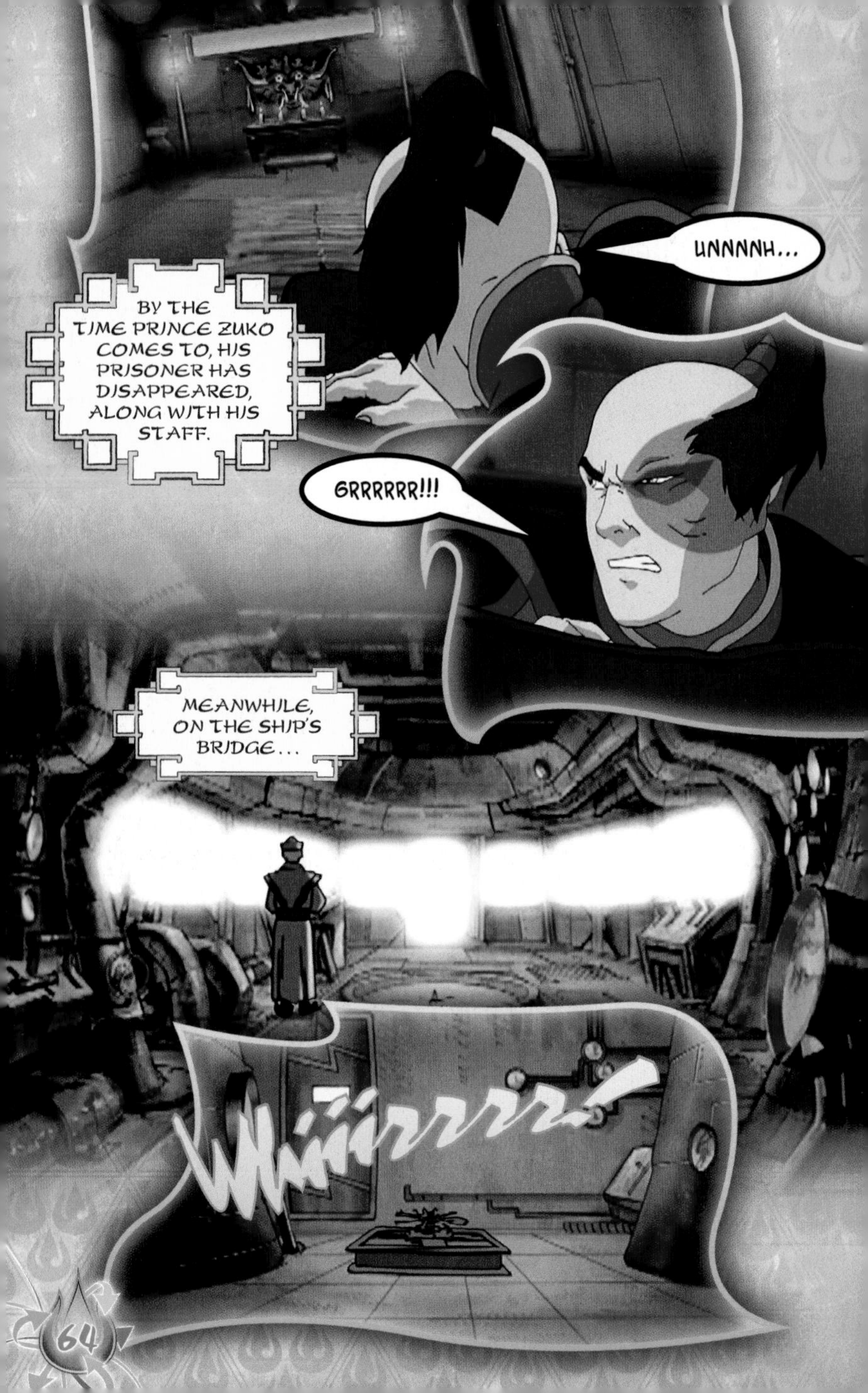
UNNNNH...
BY THE TIME PRINCE ZUKO COMES TO, HIS PRISONER HAS DISAPPEARED, ALONG WITH HIS STAFF.
GRRRRRR!!!
MEANWHILE, ON THE SHIP'S BRIDGE...
Whiiirrrrr!

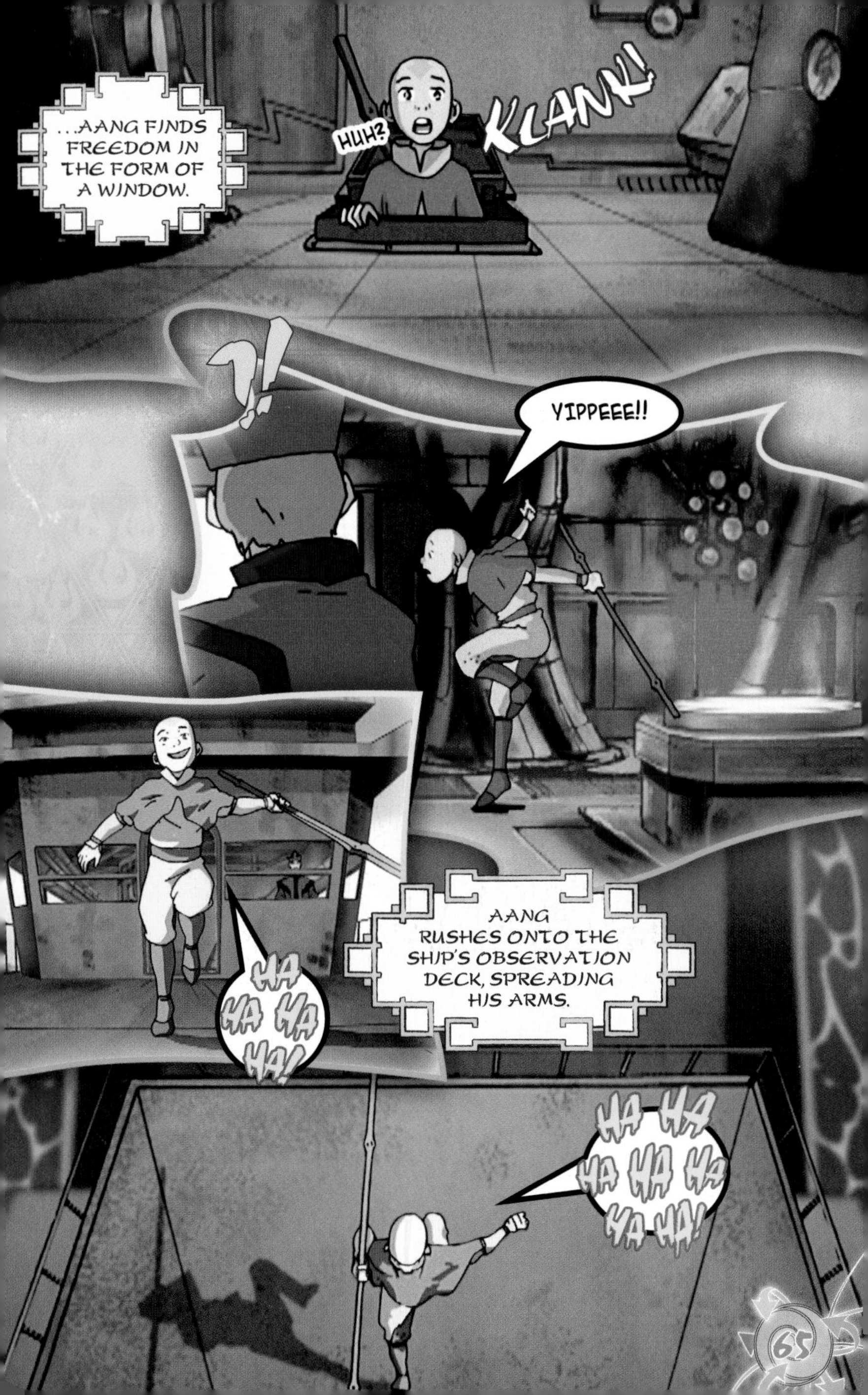
...AANG FINDS FREEDOM IN THE FORM OF A WINDOW.
HUH?
KLANK!
?!
YIPPEEE!!
HA HA HA HA!
AANG RUSHES ONTO THE SHIP'S OBSERVATION DECK, SPREADING HIS ARMS.
HA HA HA HA HA HA HA!

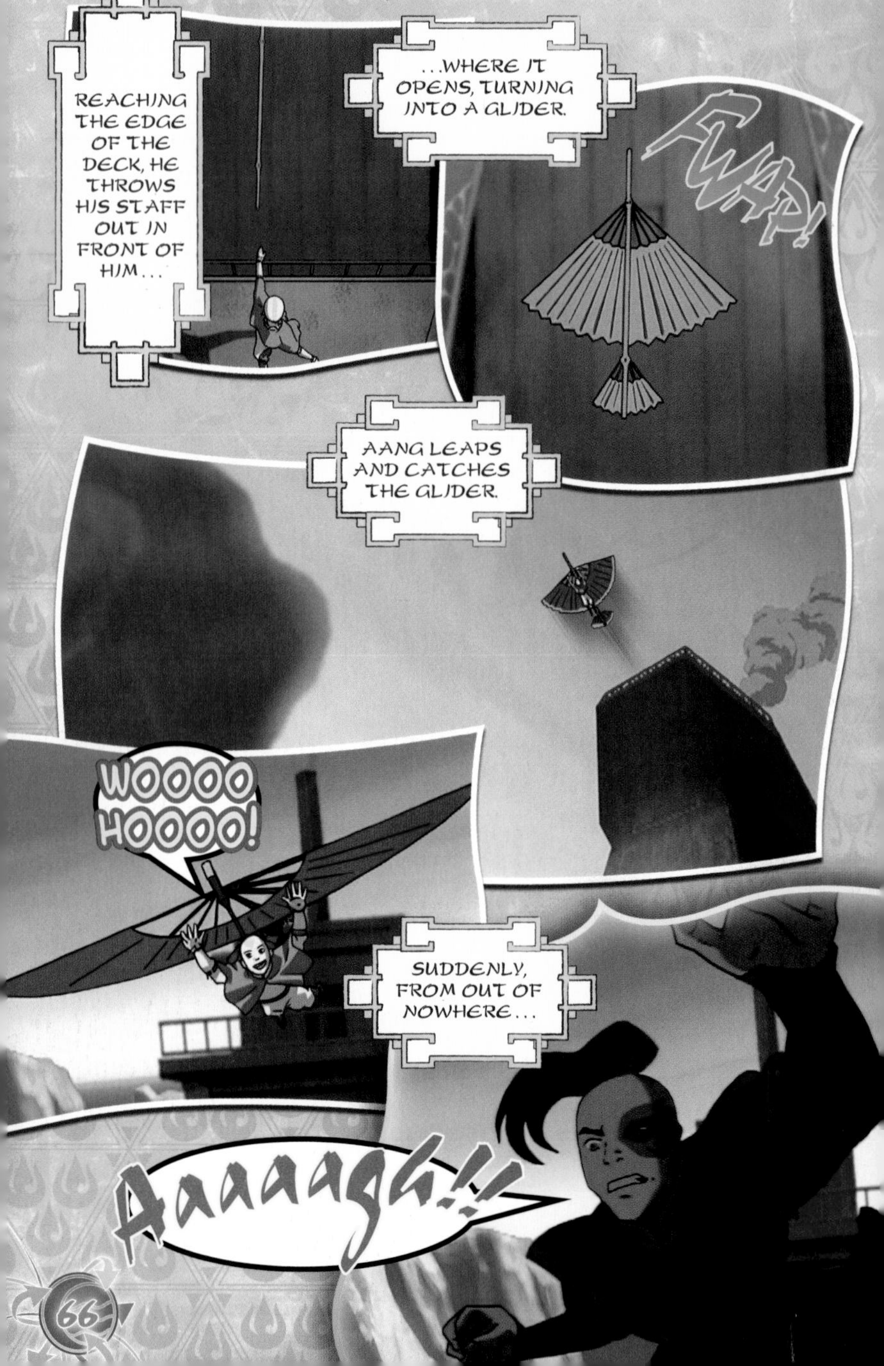
REACHING THE EDGE OF THE DECK, HE THROWS HIS STAFF OUT IN FRONT OF HIM . . .
. . .WHERE IT OPENS, TURNING INTO A GLIDER.
FWAP!
AANG LEAPS AND CATCHES THE GLIDER.
WOOOO HOOOO!
SUDDENLY, FROM OUT OF NOWHERE . . .
Aaaaagh!!

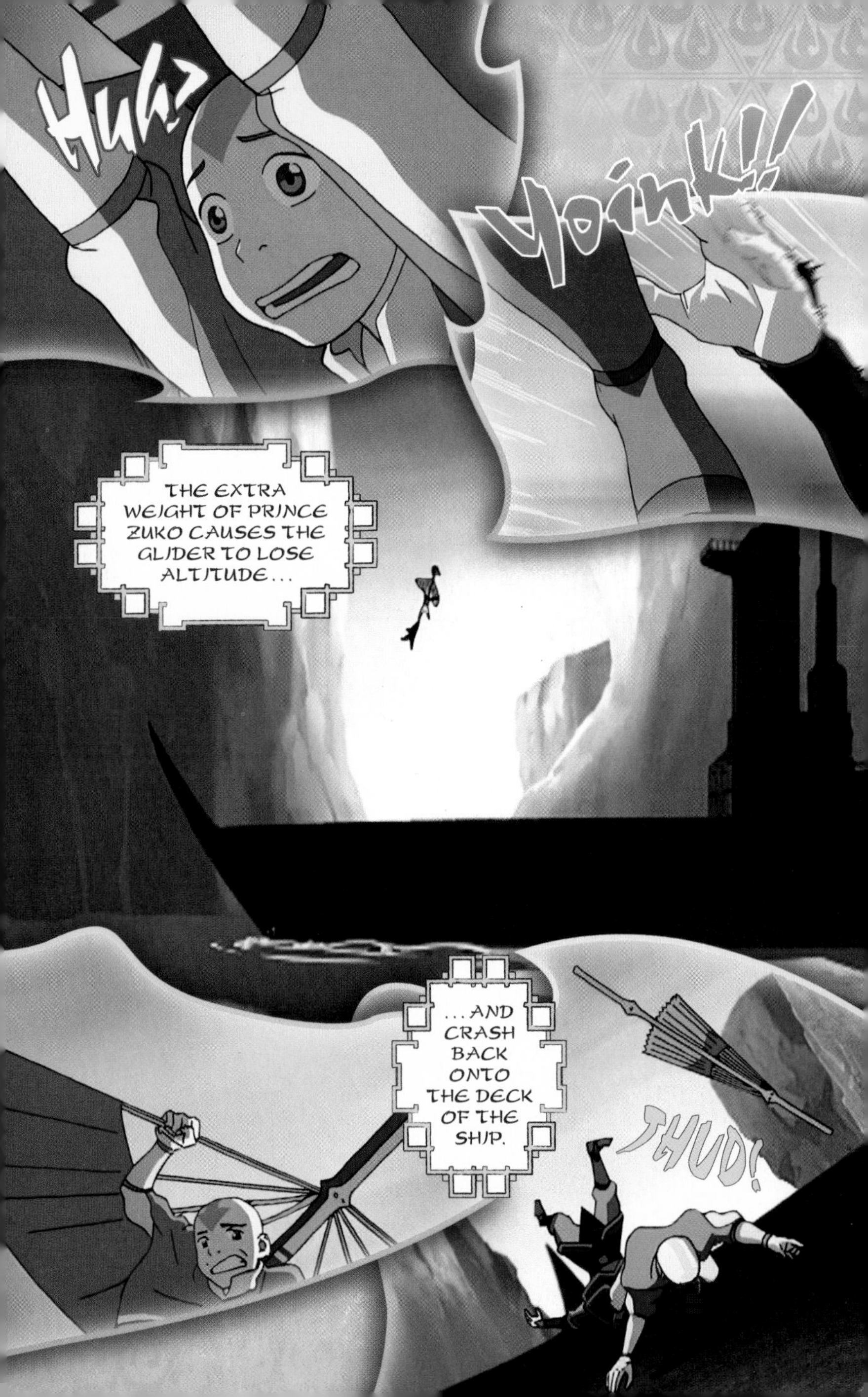
HUH?
YOINK!!
THE EXTRA WEIGHT OF PRINCE ZUKO CAUSES THE GLIDER TO LOSE ALTITUDE . . .
. . . AND CRASH BACK ONTO THE DECK OF THE SHIP.
THUD!

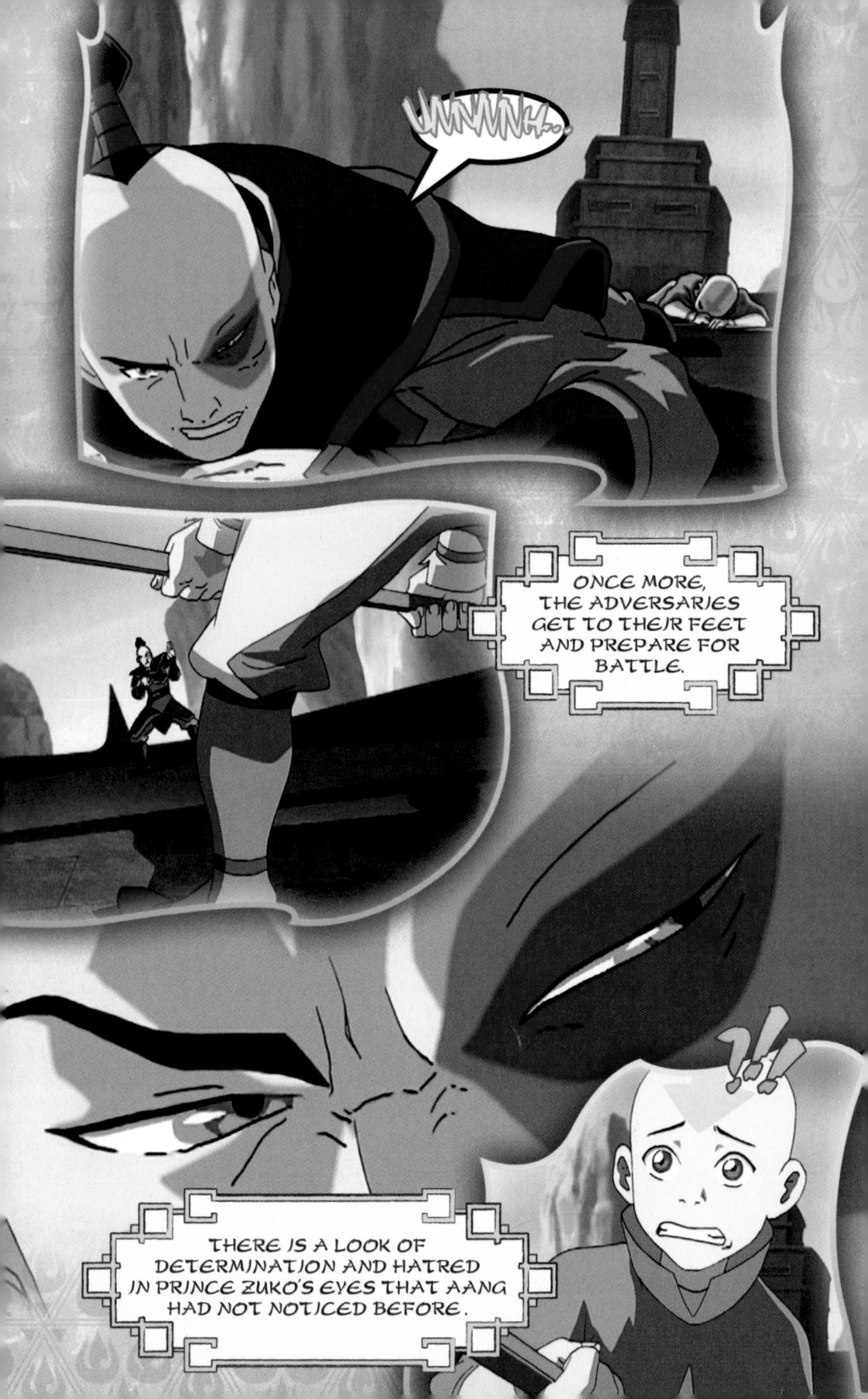
UNNNNH...
ONCE MORE, THE ADVERSARIES GET TO THEIR FEET AND PREPARE FOR BATTLE.
THERE IS A LOOK OF DETERMINATION AND HATRED IN PRINCE ZUKO'S EYES THAT AANG HAD NOT NOTICED BEFORE.

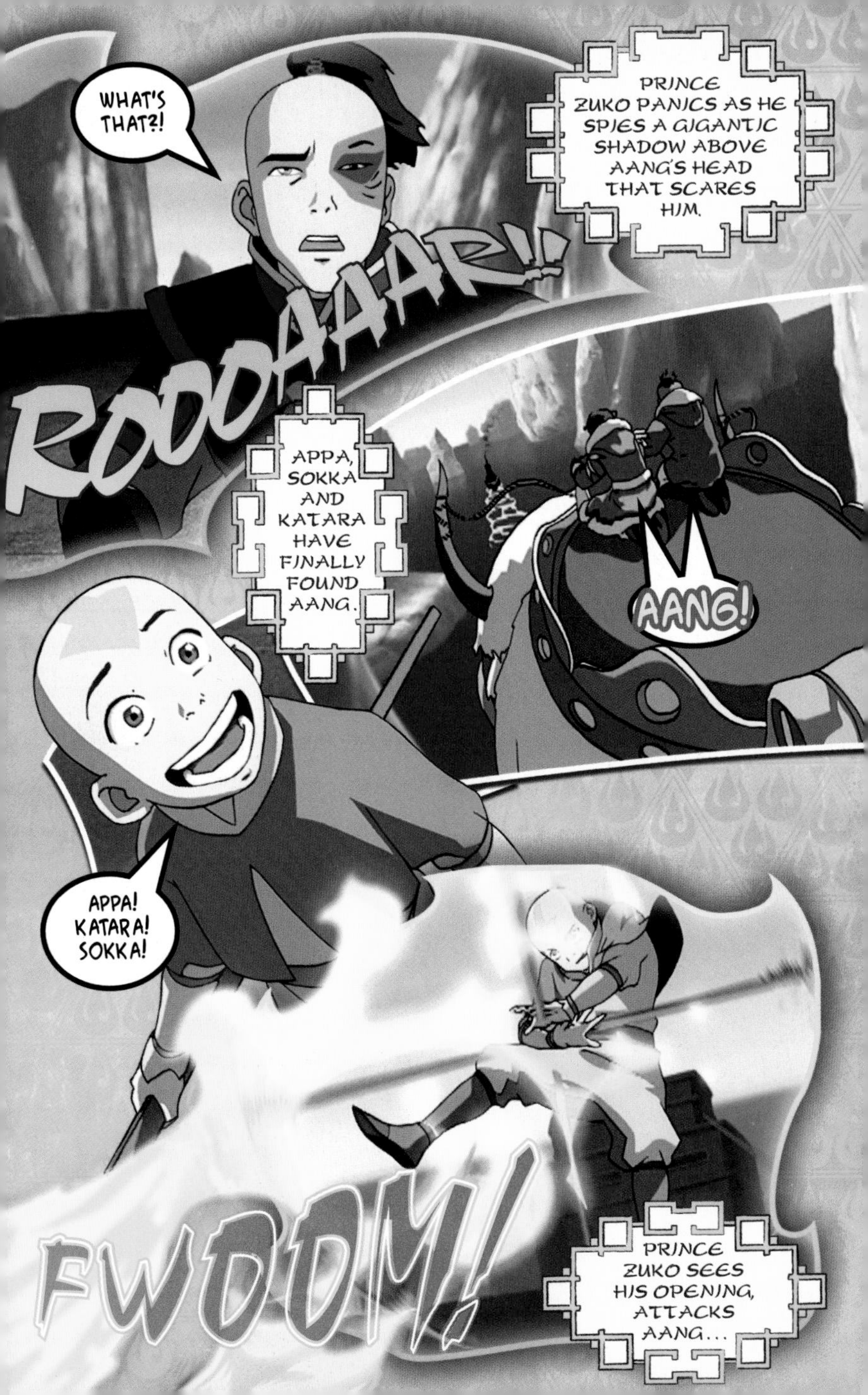
WHAT'S THAT?!
PRINCE ZUKO PANICS AS HE SPIES A GIGANTIC SHADOW ABOVE AANG'S HEAD THAT SCARES HIM.
ROOOAAAR!!
APPA, SOKKA AND KATARA HAVE FINALLY FOUND AANG.
AANG!
APPA! KATARA! SOKKA!
FWOOM!
PRINCE ZUKO SEES HIS OPENING, ATTACKS AANG...

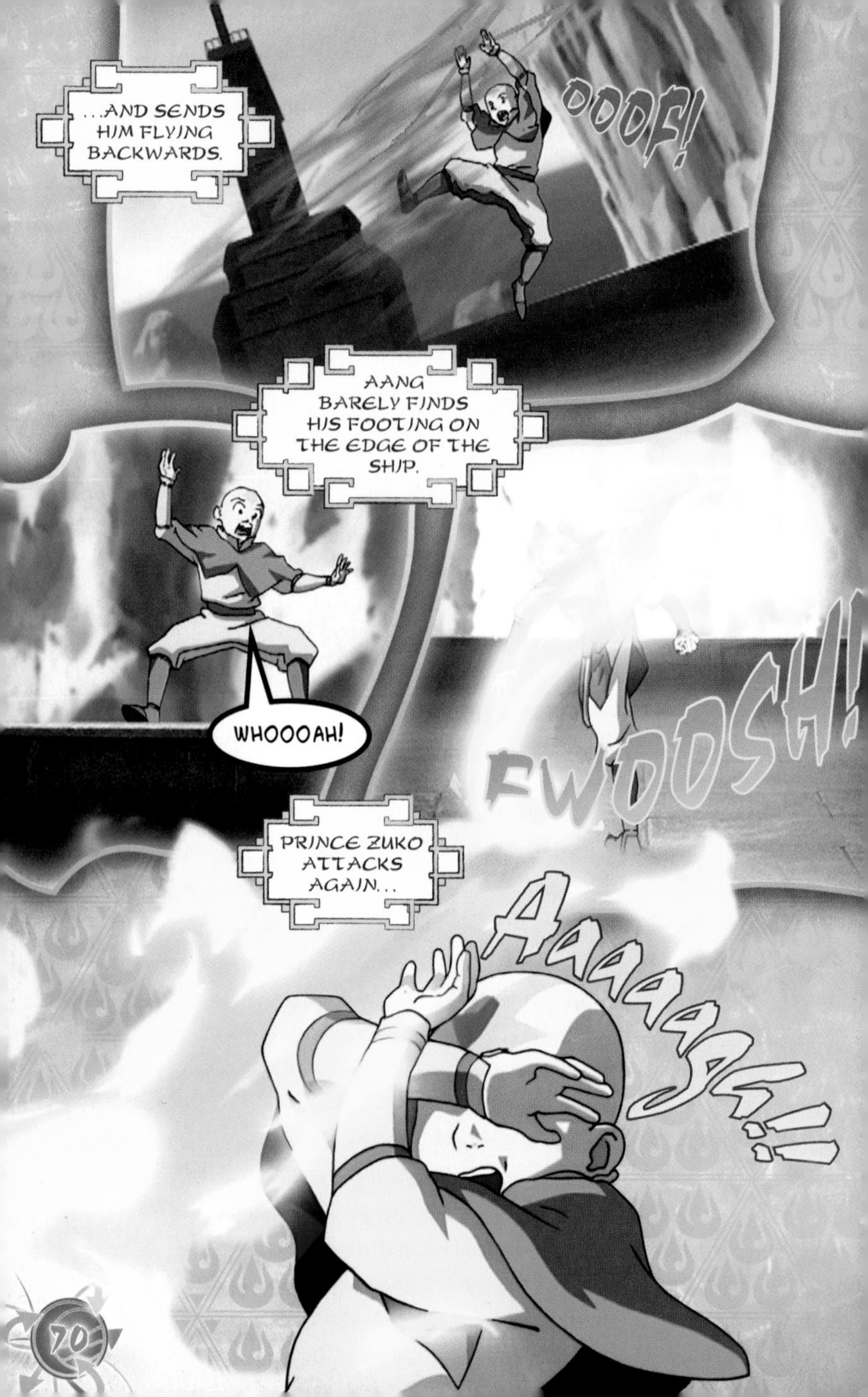

...AND SENDS HIM FLYING BACKWARDS.
OOOF!
AANG BARELY FINDS HIS FOOTING ON THE EDGE OF THE SHIP.
WHOOOAH!
FWOOSH!
PRINCE ZUKO ATTACKS AGAIN...
Aaaaagh!!!

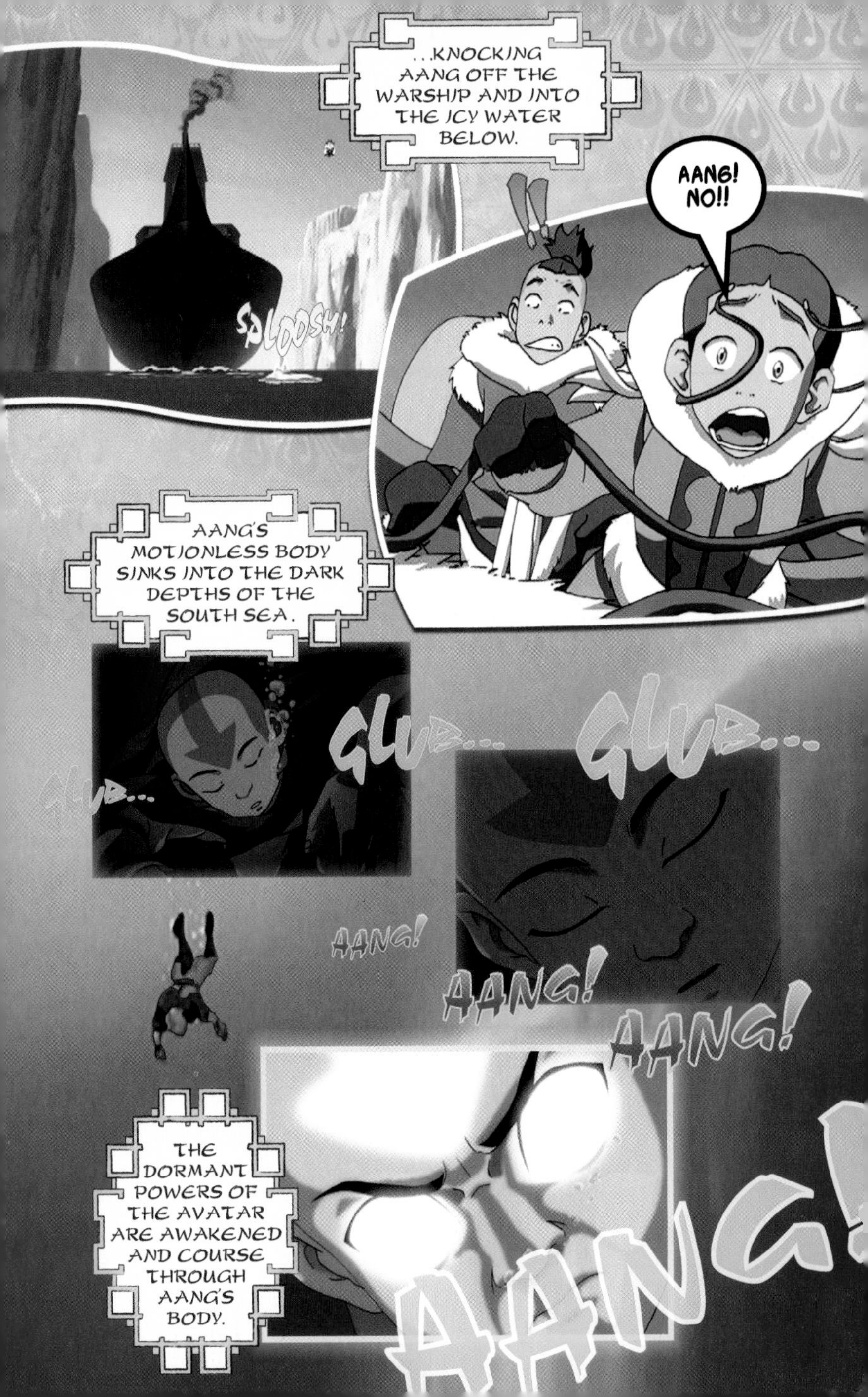
...KNOCKING AANG OFF THE WARSHIP AND INTO THE ICY WATER BELOW.
AANG! NO!!
SPLOOSH!
AANG'S MOTIONLESS BODY SINKS INTO THE DARK DEPTHS OF THE SOUTH SEA.
GLUB...
GLUB...
GLUB...
AANG!
AANG!
AANG!
AANG!
THE DORMANT POWERS OF THE AVATAR ARE AWAKENED AND COURSE THROUGH AANG'S BODY.

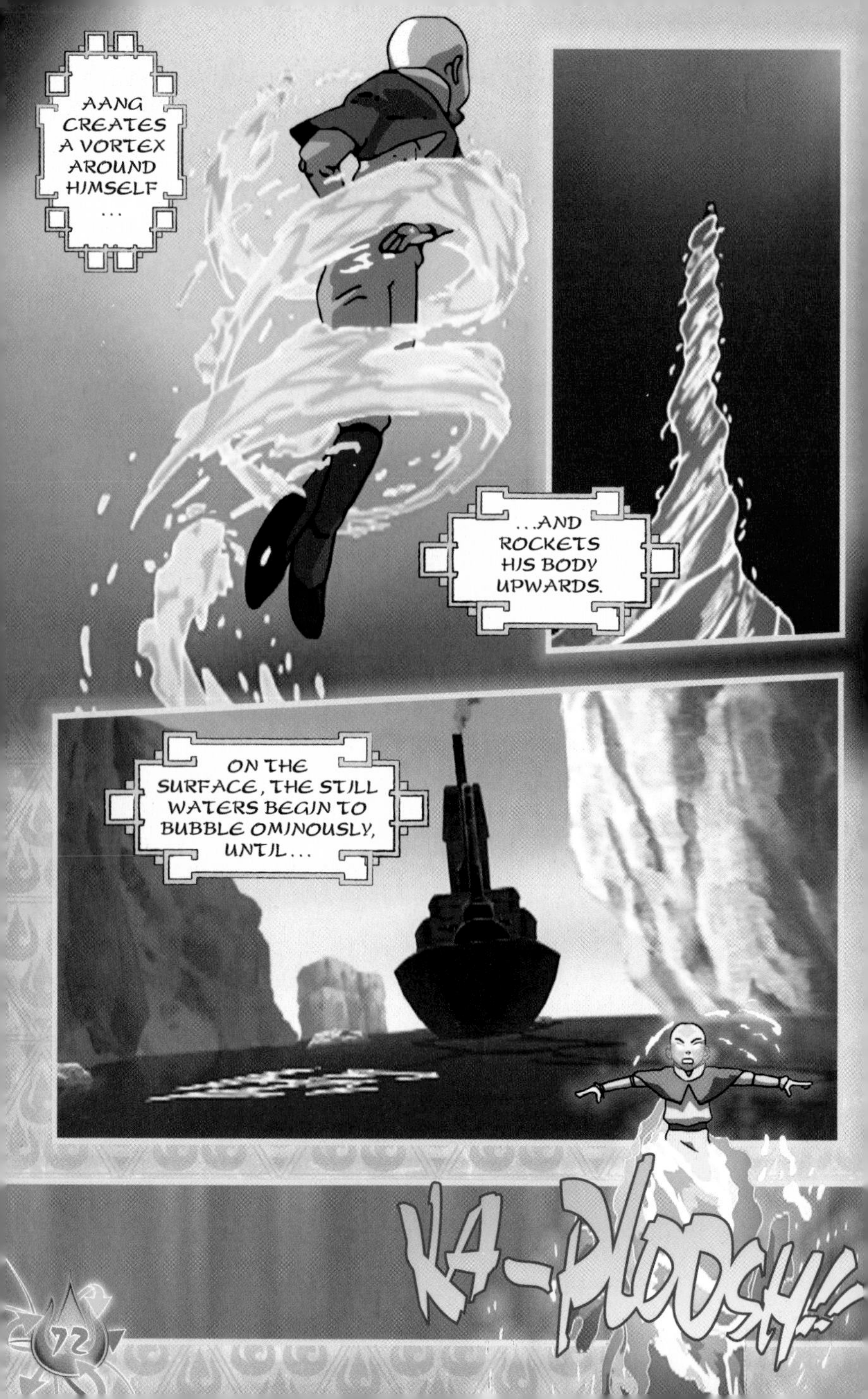
AANG CREATES A VORTEX AROUND HIMSELF . . .
. . .AND ROCKETS HIS BODY UPWARDS.
ON THE SURFACE, THE STILL WATERS BEGIN TO BUBBLE OMINOUSLY, UNTIL . . .
KA-PLOOSH!!

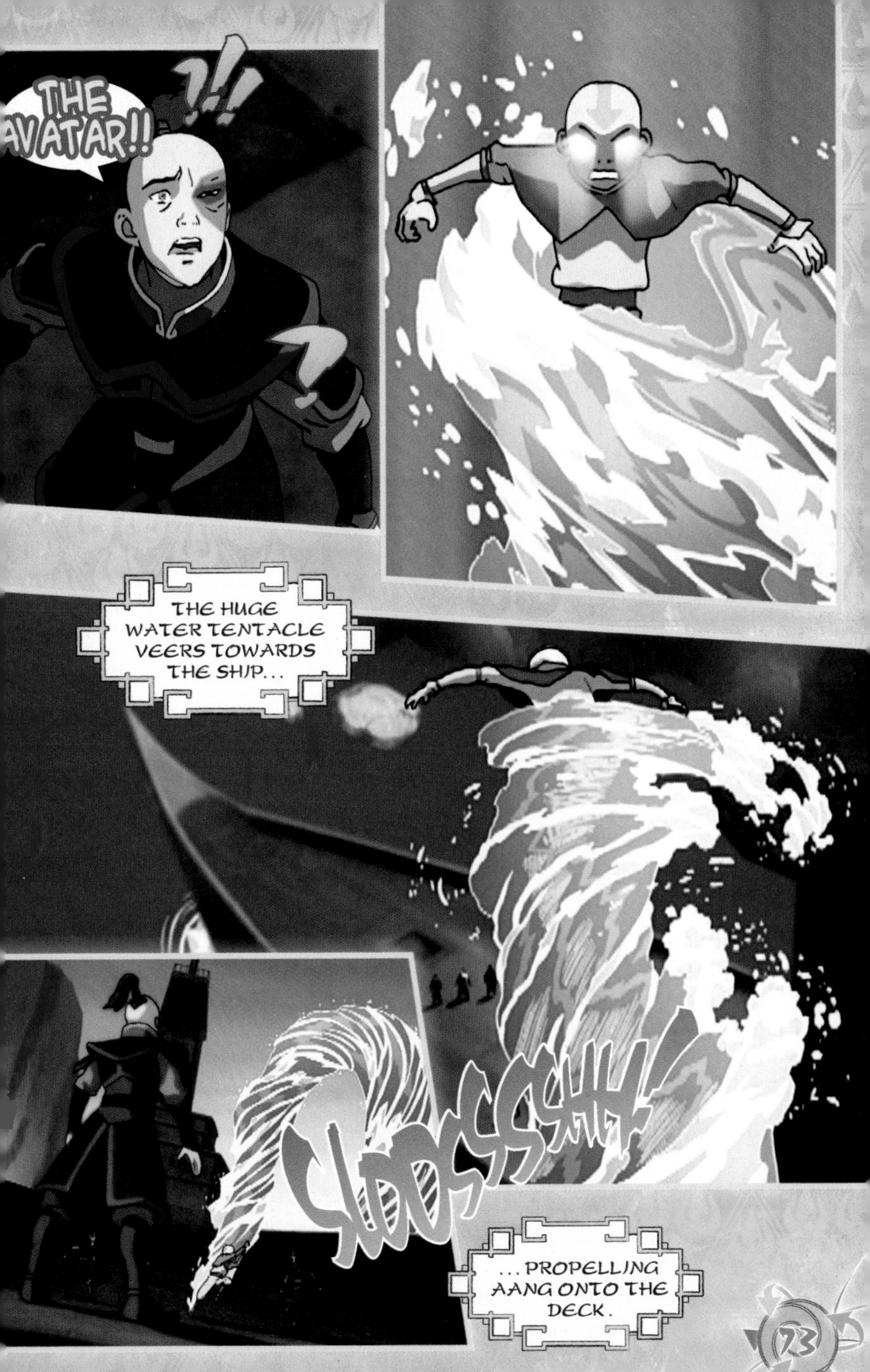
THE AVATAR!!
?!!
THE HUGE WATER TENTACLE VEERS TOWARDS THE SHIP...
...PROPELLING AANG ONTO THE DECK.

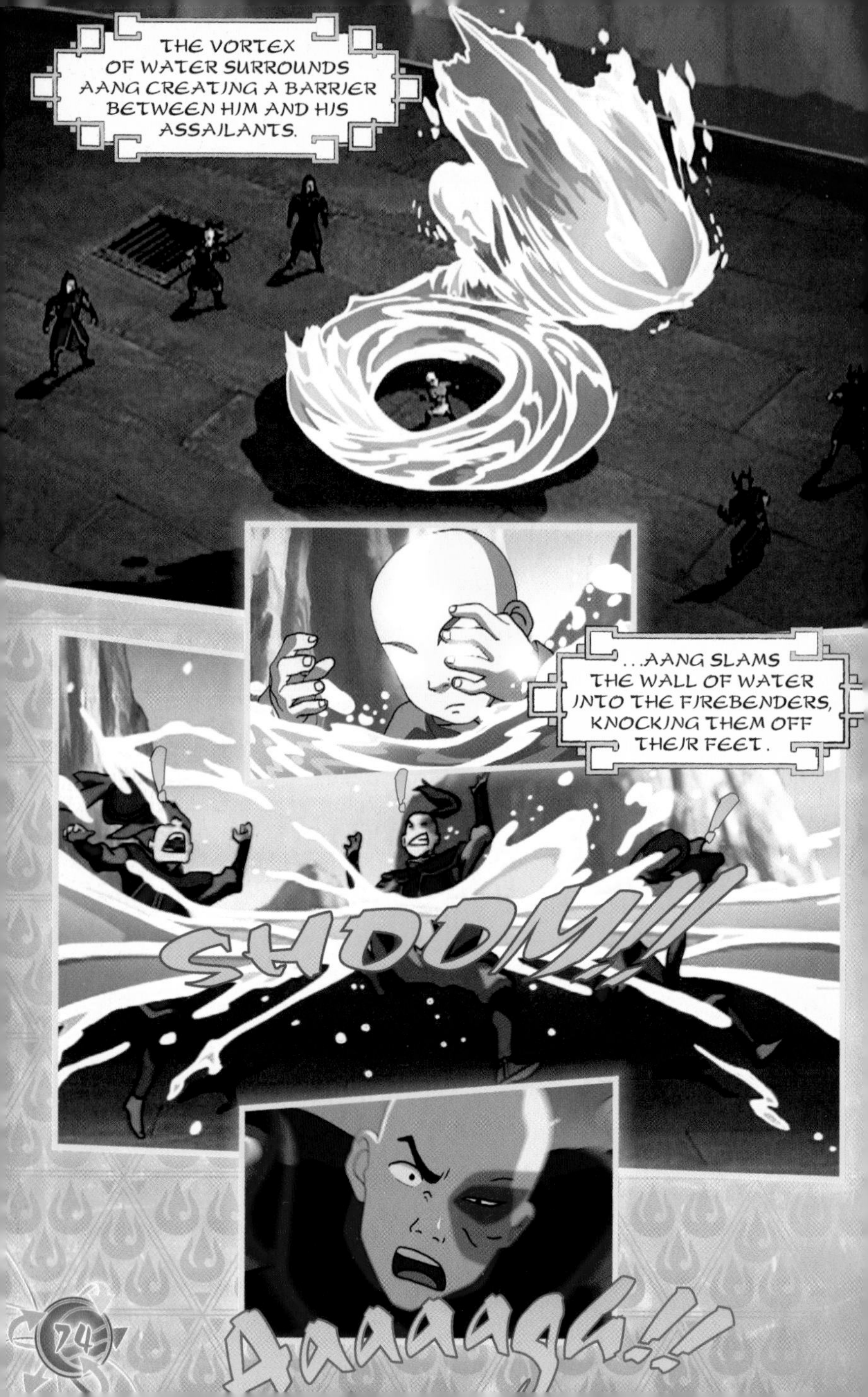
THE VORTEX OF WATER SURROUNDS AANG CREATING A BARRIER BETWEEN HIM AND HIS ASSAILANTS.
...AANG SLAMS THE WALL OF WATER INTO THE FIREBENDERS, KNOCKING THEM OFF THEIR FEET.
!
!
!
SHOOM!!
Aaaaagh!!

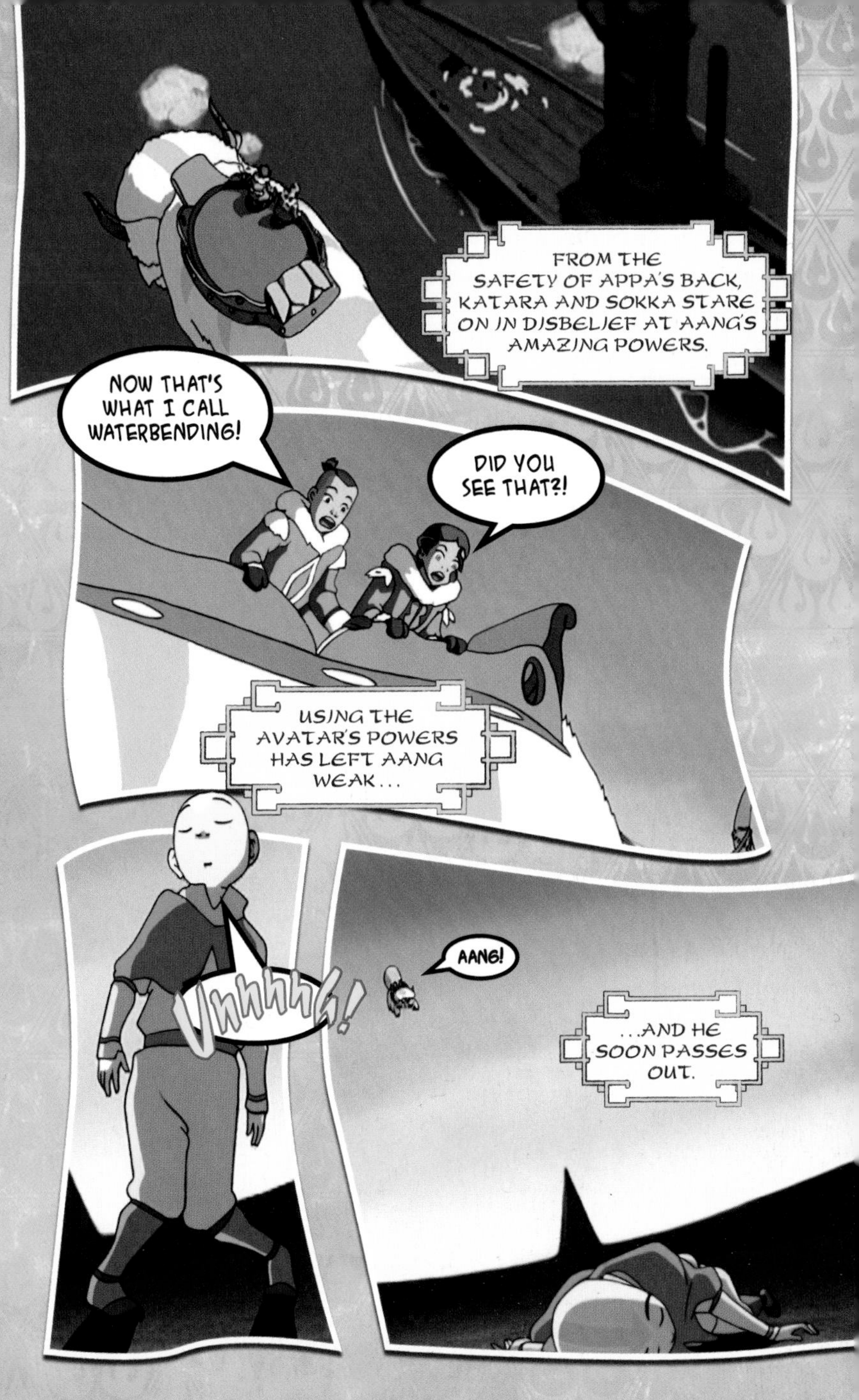

FROM THE SAFETY OF APPA'S BACK, KATARA AND SOKKA STARE ON IN DISBELIEF AT AANG'S AMAZING POWERS.
NOW THAT'S WHAT I CALL WATERBENDING!
DID YOU SEE THAT?!
USING THE AVATAR'S POWERS HAS LEFT AANG WEAK...
Unhhhh!
AANG!
...AND HE SOON PASSES OUT.

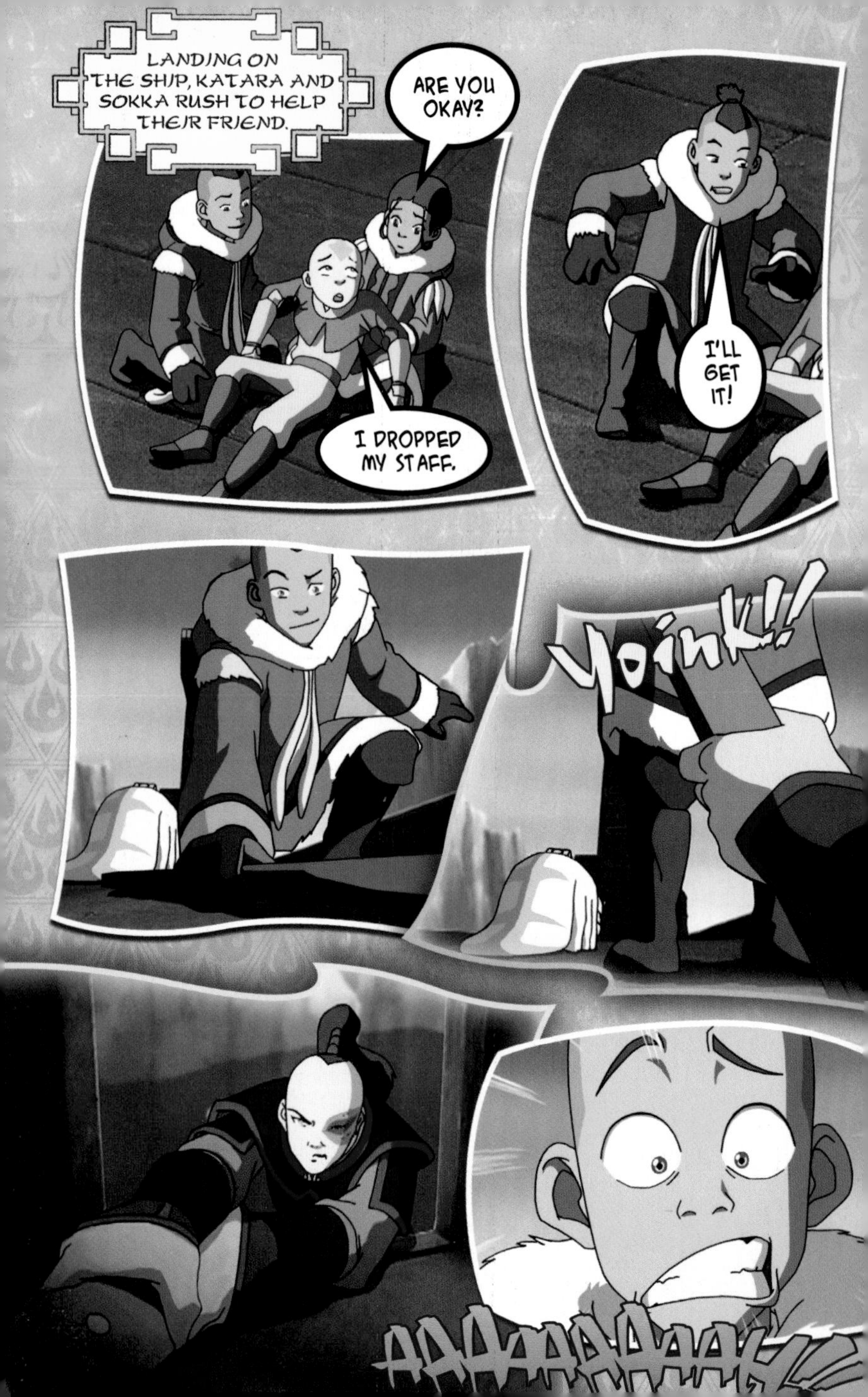
LANDING ON THE SHIP, KATARA AND SOKKA RUSH TO HELP THEIR FRIEND.
ARE YOU OKAY?
I DROPPED MY STAFF.
I'LL GET IT!
YOINK!!
AAAAAAAAAK!

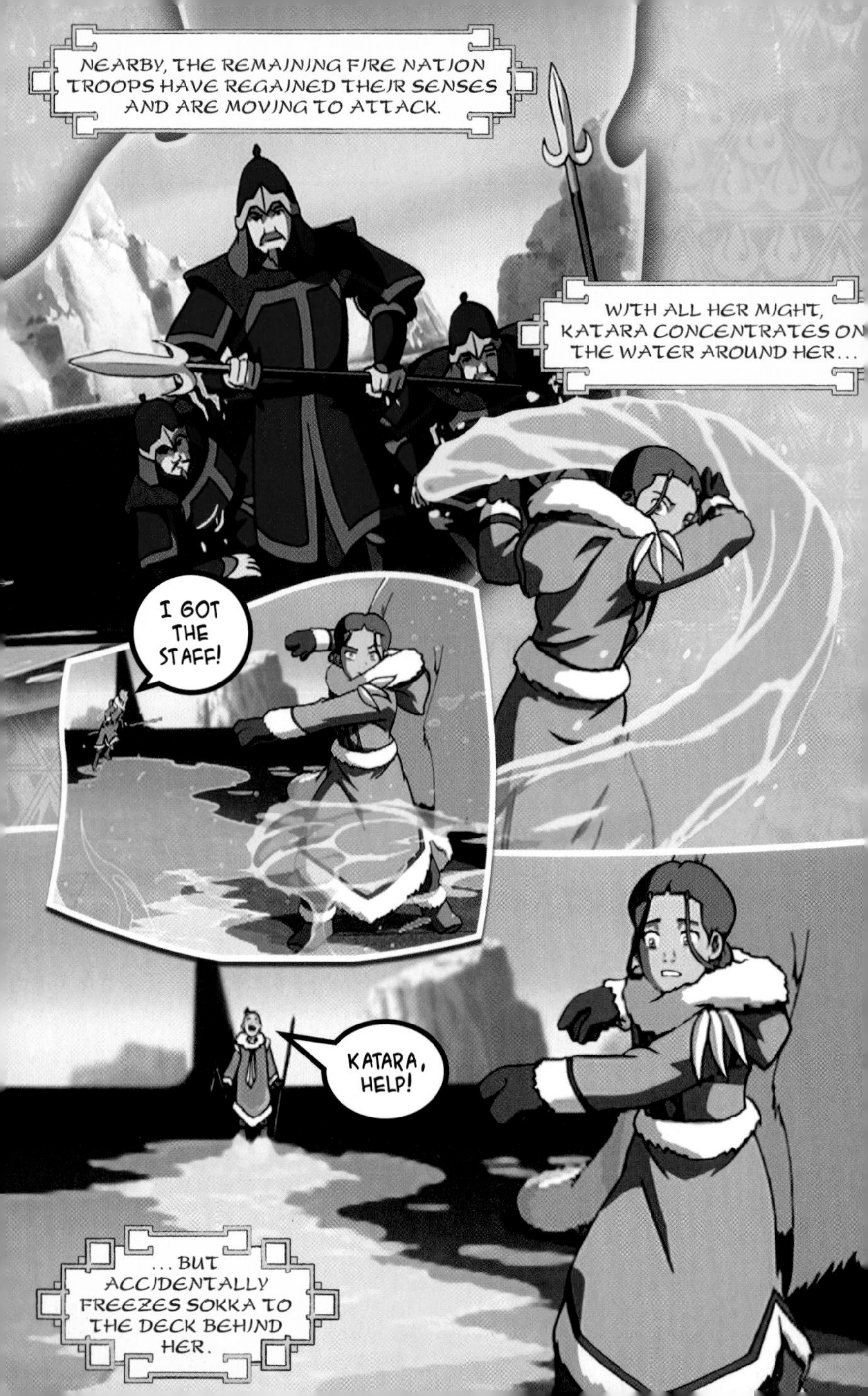
NEARBY, THE REMAINING FIRE NATION TROOPS HAVE REGAINED THEIR SENSES AND ARE MOVING TO ATTACK.
WITH ALL HER MIGHT, KATARA CONCENTRATES ON THE WATER AROUND HER...
I GOT THE STAFF!
KATARA, HELP!
...BUT ACCIDENTALLY FREEZES SOKKA TO THE DECK BEHIND HER.

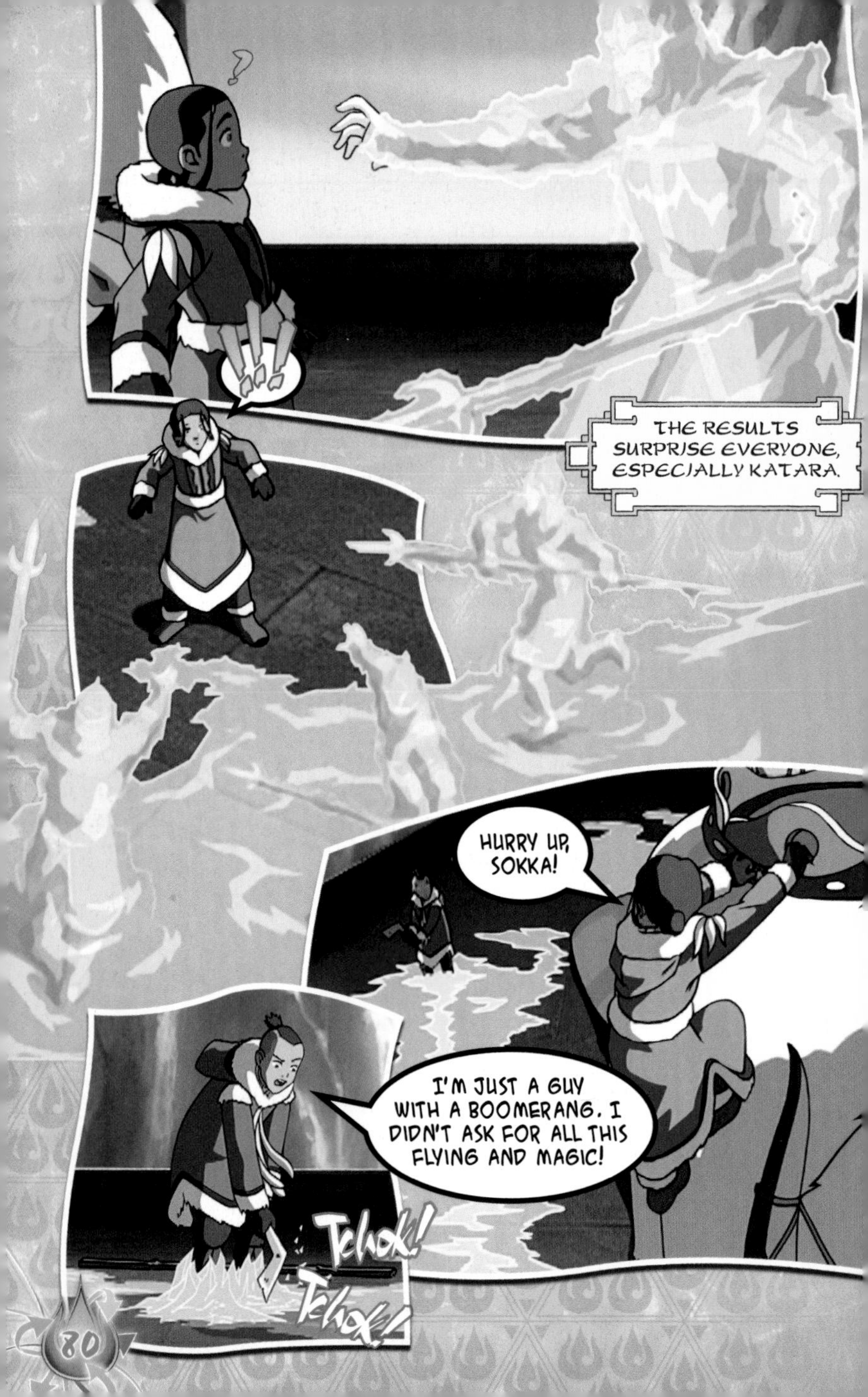
?
THE RESULTS SURPRISE EVERYONE, ESPECIALLY KATARA.
HURRY UP, SOKKA!
I'M JUST A GUY WITH A BOOMERANG. I DIDN'T ASK FOR ALL THIS FLYING AND MAGIC!
Tchok! Tchok!

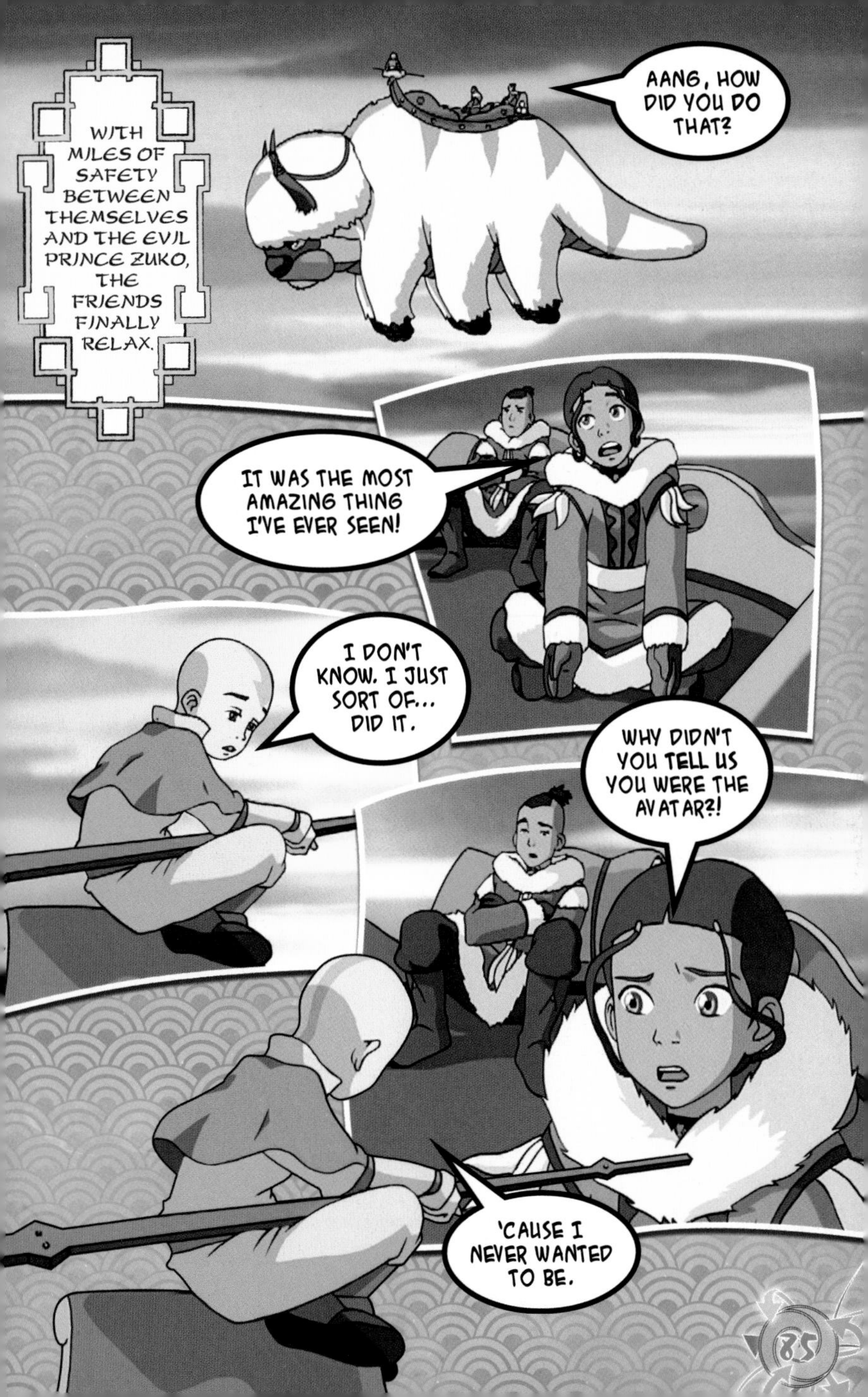
WITH MILES OF SAFETY BETWEEN THEMSELVES AND THE EVIL PRINCE ZUKO, THE FRIENDS FINALLY RELAX.
AANG, HOW DID YOU DO THAT?
IT WAS THE MOST AMAZING THING I'VE EVER SEEN!
I DON'T KNOW. I JUST SORT OF... DID IT.
WHY DIDN'T YOU TELL US YOU WERE THE AVATAR?!
'CAUSE I NEVER WANTED TO BE.

ANIMALS OF AVATAR

FLYING BISON

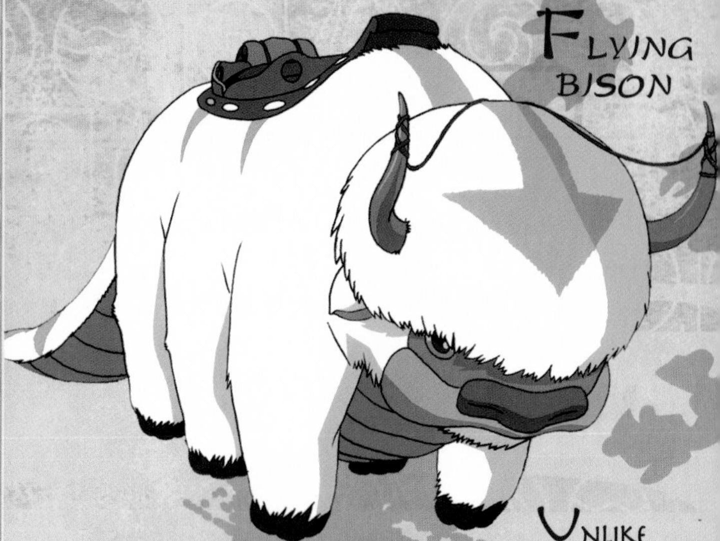

UNLIKE THE COMMON BISON, FLYING BISON ARE CONSIDERABLY LARGER WITH LIGHT TAN FUR AND DARK STRIPES ON THEIR BACKS AS WELL AS AN ARROW MARKING ON THEIR HEADS. THEY ALSO HAVE VERY BROAD TAILS WHICH THEY USE TO POWER AND STEER THEMSELVES IN THE WATER AND THE AIR. DUE TO THEIR ENORMOUS SIZE, THEY CANNOT FLY FOR LONG PERIODS OF TIME, OFTEN NEEDING TO STOP AND REST.

PENGUINS

FOUND IN ABUNDANCE ALL OVER THE NORTH AND SOUTH POLES, PENGUINS ARE DOCILE ANIMALS WITH AN INSATIABLE APPETITE FOR FISH, AND ALTHOUGH THEY HAVE TWO SETS OF WINGS THEY CANNOT FLY. SHY, YET FRIENDLY, THEY TEND TO AVOID CONTACT WITH HUMANS ALTHOUGH THEY HAVE BEEN KNOWN TO ALLOW PEOPLE TO USE THEM AS SLEDS FOR THE PRICE OF A FISH.

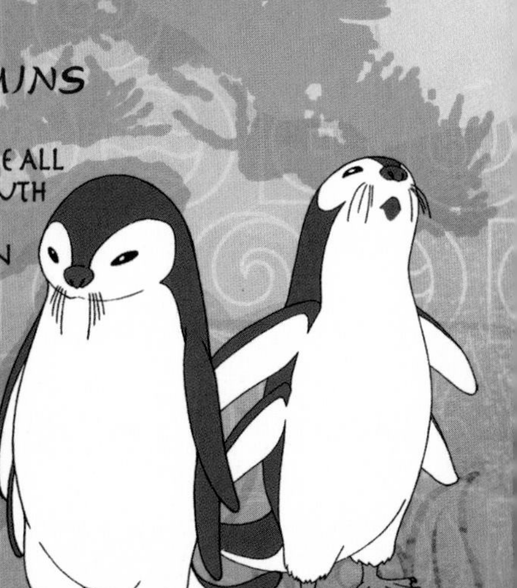

Winged Lemurs

Looking like a cross between a spotted bat and a black and white lemur, these creatures are extremely intelligent and have highly developed senses of hearing and smell. They can be trained, but if there is food nearby, they will eat it, even if they are told not to. Winged lemurs are nervous creatures; they panic easily and will screech in fear if they feel threatened.

Zebra Seals

Zebra seals get their name from the distinctive striping on their backs, which they use to camouflage their numbers from predators while swimming or hunting for fish. Zebra seals live together in small groups and avoid contact with other animals whenever possible.

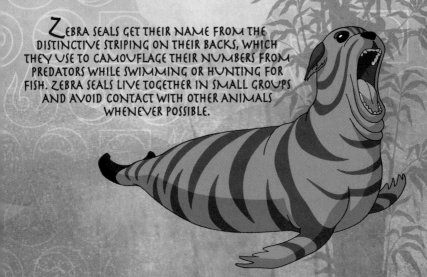

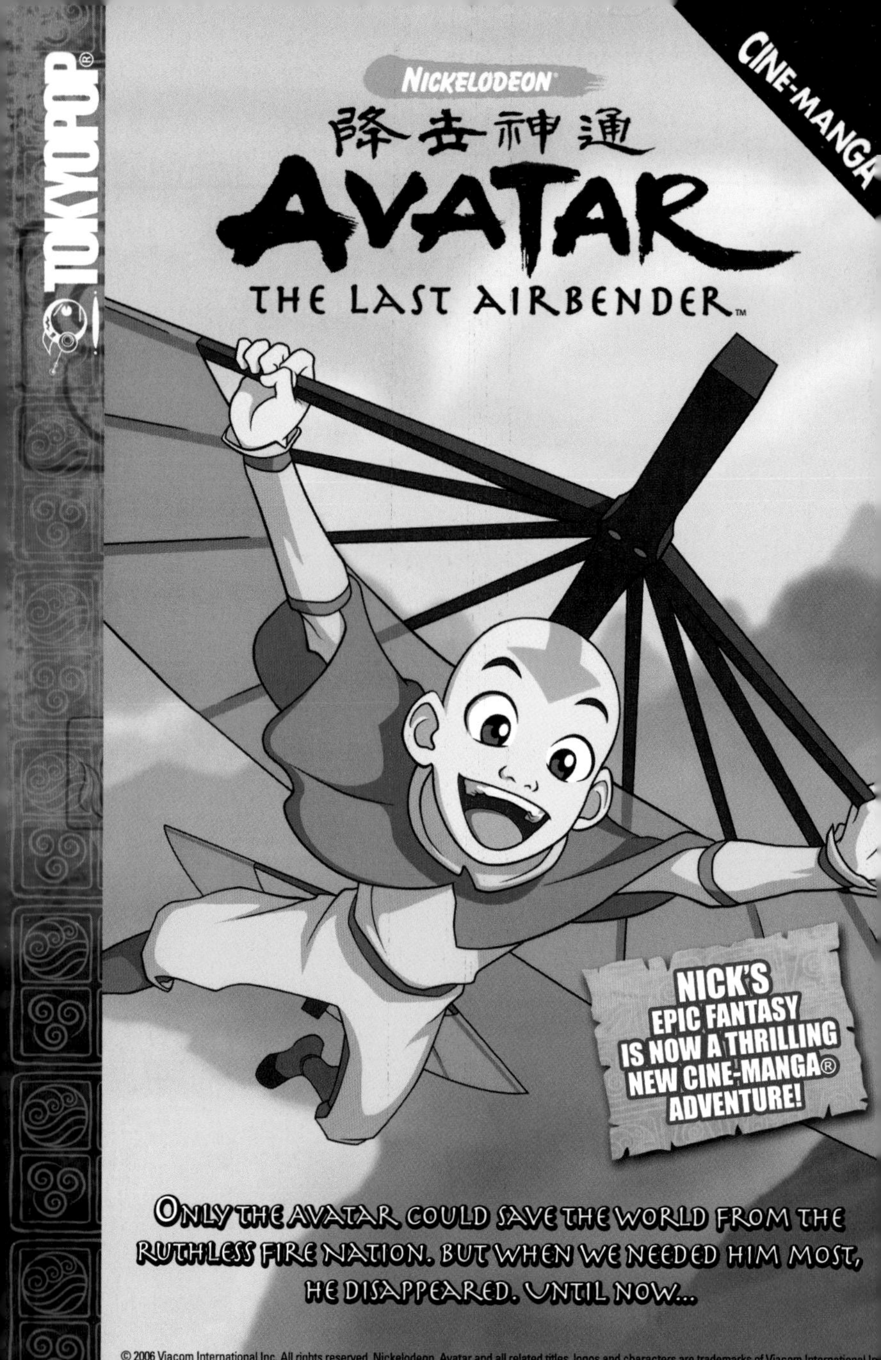
TOKYOPOP®
CINE-MANGA
NICKELODEON
降世神通
AVATAR
THE LAST AIRBENDER™
NICK'S EPIC FANTASY IS NOW A THRILLING NEW CINE-MANGA® ADVENTURE!
ONLY THE AVATAR COULD SAVE THE WORLD FROM THE RUTHLESS FIRE NATION. BUT WHEN WE NEEDED HIM MOST, HE DISAPPEARED. UNTIL NOW...

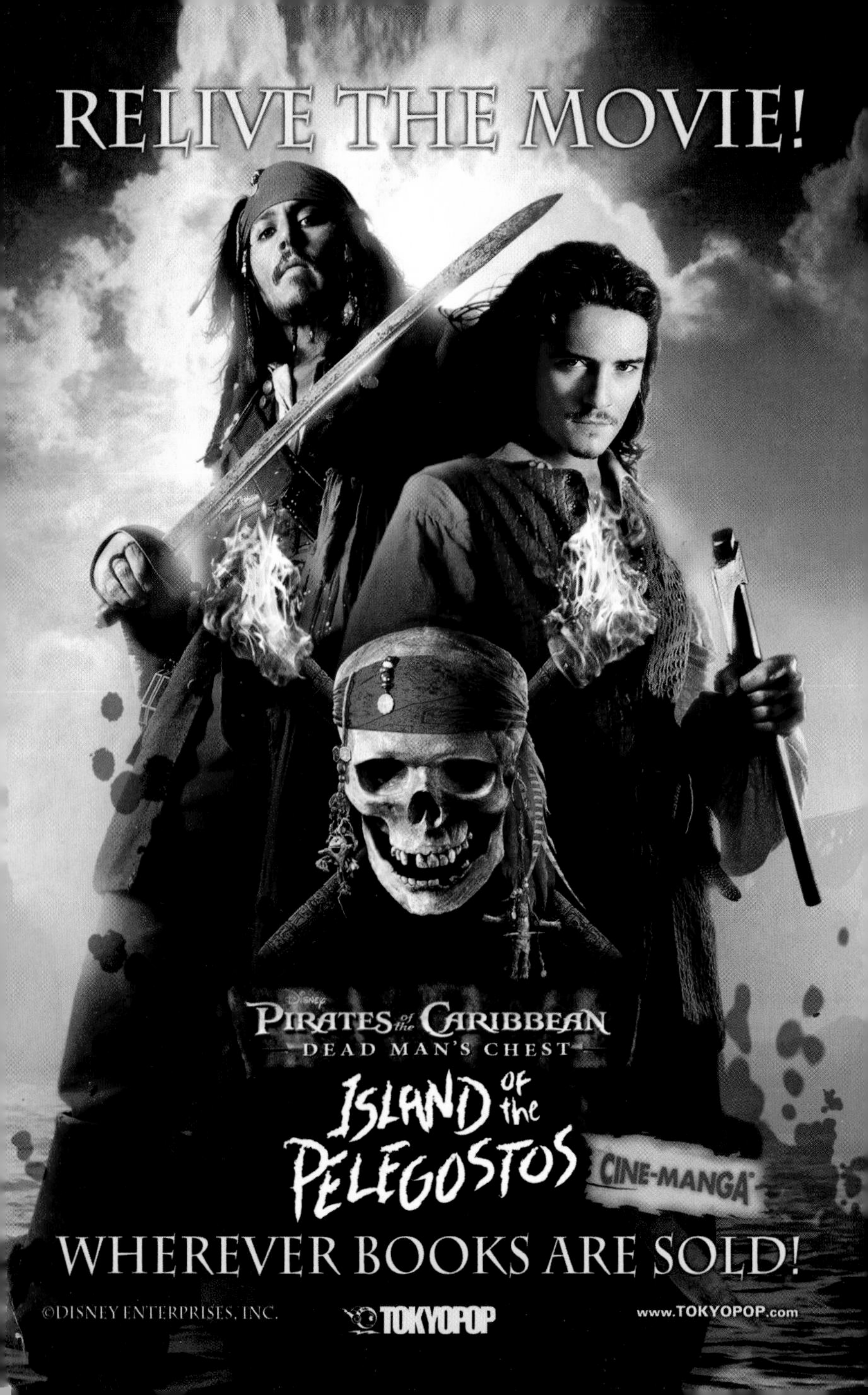